James M. (James Montgomery) Bailey

Mr. Philips` goneness

James M. (James Montgomery) Bailey

Mr. Philips` goneness

ISBN/EAN: 9783743303287

Manufactured in Europe, USA, Canada, Australia, Japa

Cover: Foto ©ninafisch / pixelio.de

Manufactured and distributed by brebook publishing software
(www.brebook.com)

James M. (James Montgomery) Bailey

Mr. Philips` goneness

MR. PHILLIPS' GONENESS.

BY

JAMES M. BAILEY,

"THE DANBURY-NEWS MAN,"

AUTHOR OF "ENGLAND FROM A BACK-WINDOW," "LIFE IN DANBURY,"
"THEY ALL DO IT," ETC.

———•———

BOSTON:
LEE AND SHEPARD, PUBLISHERS.
NEW YORK:
CHARLES T. DILLINGHAM.
1879.

A CONCILIATORY WORD.

DEAR READER, this is a simple story, simply told. It is not designed to excite, but to improve. If it is not attractive, it is because it is true, and finds a cruel emphasis all about you. If the little volume should make a single husband more tender, a single wife more patient, and sell well, I will feel that my labor has not been in vain.

Yours sincerely,

THE AUTHOR.

CONTENTS.

MR. PHILLIPS' GONENESS

THE STORY OF A WEDDED LOVE.

CHAPTER I.

THE NEW JOURNEYMAN.

GALLOWHILL, two hours' ride by rail from Boston, boasted one paper, — "The Gazette." "The Gazette" was published every Tuesday, at two dollars per annum, strictly in advance, as is customary with village newspapers. The office of "The Gazette" was on the second floor of a two-story brick block on Main Street. The office was approached by a stairway from the street, which stairway led directly into the printing-room, without the preface of a hall, and, so communicating with no other portion of the second floor, was devoted exclusively to the uses of "The Gazette" and its patrons. On the risers to the steps were placards in bold black type, setting forth the name of the paper, and the fact that the art preservative was carefully manipulated in all its

7

branches. On the steps were various accumulations of dust, reverently spared by the broom, which semi-weekly passed down the middle of the way;—bits of printed paper twisted into wads, and smeared with ink, and bits of white and colored papers, the refuse of the cutter, either dragged there by the all-comprehensive feet of rural visitors, or dropped there by children coming away with supplies for their own use.

The plastered walls on either side were smeared with ink, in designs having no intelligible significance, and in designs with plenty of significance. Who made these marks, no one knew: furthermore, no one could tell when they were done. They are common to all stairways approaching country printing-offices, attracting no comment, and stimulating no research. The editor of " The Gazette" supposed, when he gave the matter any thought at all, that they were laid on by the plasterer when the walls were made; an extremely natural supposition, and, likely enough, the only reasonable one possible.

There was a board partition enclosing the stairway opening, with a door at the head. This improvement had been made by the present editor of "The Gazette." For the many years preceding his coming, the business of the office had required no door, and simply a rail in place of the partition, to keep anxious subscribers and abstracted contributors from backing off, and imperilling the panelling of the street-door.

The printing-office was an almost square apartment, with very little spare room, all space having been intelligently economized. There were the racks for the cases of type, so arranged as to command the best light; the imposing-stones; a hand-press for printing the paper; two treadle-presses for job-work; and the various machinery and appliances common to a country printing-office. A prominent feature was a rusted stove, with draught always opened to its fullest capacity. It has come to be doubted if it is possible to modify the draught to a country printing-office stove; and, whatever may be the pattern of the article, this dreadful peculiarity seems to be either built into it at its inception, or ingrafted thereon by some invisible process when it is set up. It is because of this that a country printing-office consumes more coal than a blacksmith-shop. It is a most astounding phenomenon.

The sanctum of "The Gazette" was indicated by a desk and a chair, both over the stairway, and lighted by one of the three front windows.

It was on a Monday evening in January, 1876. Three gas-jets were burning in the office of "The Gazette." One of them was over the editorial desk; another was over a rack in the rear of the room; and the third lighted an imposing-stone. The shades over these jets were admirable in concentrating the light upon the objects beneath them, but threw the greater part of the room into deep shadow. The stove was red all round with the tremendous effort it was making to impart the least amount of heat with the greatest amount of coal.

A tall, slim man was at work at the rack under the gas-jet. Occasionally he would pass to the lighted stone, adjust a line in the form resting thereon, and then return. He worked and moved silently, and in passing to and fro would lose himself in the shadow, only to re-appear in the light with startling abruptness.

At the desk sat Thomas B. Griggs, editor of "The Gallowhill Gazette," and "plain and ornamental job-printer," as the advertisement on the left hand of the title-page of the paper, and various bill-heads, letter-heads, and cards on the desk, indicated. He was a young man, scarcely thirty, with a shapely head, curly brown hair, mustache a shade lighter than the hair, a prominent nose, — which always indicates depth of character and firmness of purpose to the owner and immediate relatives, — and other well-formed features. Aside from a stain of ink on the second finger of his right hand, and an abstracted air on his face, there was nothing in Mr. Griggs' appearance to inform a casual observer that he was an editor; and yet he had been at the head of "The Gazette" two whole years, and had worked faithfully upon its columns all that time. He was now hard at work preparing copy for the paper of the morrow, and he worked like one in a nervous hurry. There was a pile of newspaper clippings at his side, and close to it the trusty paste-pot; but it was with neither of these he was engaged. Several sheets of manuscript occupied his attention, and very closely held it, judging from the contraction of his brows.

"What an infernal mess!" he ejaculated.

"What's that, Tom?" asked the tall, slim man, without raising his head.

"This communication from Holcomb."

The tall, slim man lifted his head on hearing the name, and turned what would have revealed an anxious face, had the shadows permitted, toward his chief.

"You ain't agoin' to publish any of his stuff to-morrow, are you?"

"That'll depend a good deal on whether I'm able to make it out by that time," was the grim reply.

"Well, if you do, we won't get out till midnight," said the tall, slim man gloomily. "We're two columns behind now; and, if we've got to tackle his manuscript, we're up the spout sure for this week. How much is there of the infernal stuff?"

"About a column."

"Holy Moses!" gasped the tall, slim man.

The editor counted over the sheets of Mr. Holcomb's unfortunate manuscript, and said, —

"I won't use it this week. I'll tell him it got mislaid. He's an old nuisance anyway;" and with this compromising opinion the conscientious editor dropped the subject. "We ought to have another man, and I must see about it," he added.

And then he turned to the clippings, and proceeded to paste them on a slip of paper, making alterations in some of them on the margin. While thus engaged, a step was heard on the stairs.

"I wonder who on earth that can be," he pettishly thought.

The step ascended. There was a moment of fumbling about for the latch, and then the door opened, and some one entered. The new-comer saw the tall, slim man at the case; and he worked his way to him through the shadows that lay upon the racks and machinery in his way. The object desired looked up at the sound, and curiously toward the comer.

"Is the editor in?" asked the visitor.

The tall, slim man had never before heard the voice; and he looked hard at the face, to make sure that he had never before seen the owner, and then he said, —

"Yes: there he is," and pointed to the desk.

The stranger worked his way through the shadows to the place indicated; while the tall, slim man, understanding he was a stranger, made his business his own, as was eminently proper in the foreman of a country printing-office, and, dropping his work, turned his full attention upon what was going forward. The visitor, reaching Editor Griggs, set down the very thin bag he carried, and removed his hat.

As far as the light would permit, the editor saw a young man, apparently not more than twenty, with sallow features, and a restless expression to his eye that was easily noted even in the imperfect light. He wore his hair, which was black and straight, rather long; and the hat which he removed was a slouch, of which the brim, like the hair it covered, was more in quantity than the prevailing style sanctioned. His whole appearance was so strongly indicative of an intensely poetic nature, that the heart of the editor sank within him. He glanced at the rusty bag, and sighed.

"You are the editor, I believe?" suggested the stranger.

"Yes."

"I have called to see if I could find work with you at type-setting."

The revulsion of feeling in the breast of the editor that set in on the receipt of this information was too great for concealment. He half rose from the chair in the excess of his emotion.

"You want a ' sit,' eh?"

"Yes, sir."

"Are you pretty rapid?"

"Not very. I have had some two years' experience at the case, and can set pretty good; but I am not able to earn big wages."

Tom Griggs' face brightened up at this last. "The Gallowhill Gazette" was not pecuniarily in a condition to pay big wages.

"Where do you come from," he next asked.

"Boston."

"Much used to manuscript?"

"Yes, sir."

"Well, let me see," mused the editor, softly tapping the desk with his pencil. "We are pretty well pressed just at present, and could use another man to advantage; but we can't pay heavy, you know." He looked up to the face of the youth for a corroboration of this view of the situation.

"I suppose not," the stranger was so kind as to say. "I don't seek for large pay: I am willing to work for small wages; but I must have work," he added in a tone of desperation. "I have got no money; and, if I don't get something to do, I shall kill myself."

"I hope it ain't so bad as that," hastily rejoined Editor Griggs, looking intently at the sallow face. "How much wages do you want?"

"I don't want to set the price, sir. I am willing to work faithfully, and I am sure you will be satisfied with me. I thought, that, if you were willing, 1 might stay with you a week, in which time you could see what I can do, and could tell what I would be worth to you in case you wanted me longer."

"Well, that's fair enough," candidly conceded Mr. Griggs. "You can come on in the morning, I suppose?"

"Yes, sir."

"Where are you staying in town?"

"Nowhere, as yet. I came right here from the depot."

Editor Griggs turned his eyes toward the tall, slim man, who was all attention, and called, —

" Ez ! "

The tall, slim man came over at once.

" Ez, this is a young man from Boston, a type-setter, who is going to help us out for a few days. By the way, your name ? "

" Redner."

" Ah, yes ! Well, Mr. Redner, this is Mr. Phillips, the foreman of ' The Gazette.' " It is not to be denied that Mr. Griggs said this with considerable unction. It is not every country printing-office that has a foreman.

Mr. Redner extended his hand, which Mr. Phillips accepted with the awkwardness peculiar to the blending of dignity with bashfulness.

Ezekiah Phillips was not as old as his employer; but he appeared older. His eyes were large, but receding; his nose, large and progressive. It was a fully developed Roman nose, and gave to the rest of the face — especially when the owner was in a confidential mood, either from liquor or circumstances — a preternaturally solemn air. Mr. Phillips was both positive and wavering, both shrewd and credulous. When under the mellowing influences of alcohol, he was both combative and apologetic, and would give way to either a flood of tears or a torrent of profanity with equal facility ; and would blend pathos and ferocity in a remarkable manner, throwing over all a solemnity most profound. Besides being a good workman, Mr. Phillips had a strong bass voice, which was utilized to great advantage in the choir of the

Gallowhill Congregational Church at two Sunday services.

"Ez," said Editor Griggs, "Mr. Redner has just come to Gallowhill, and has no place to stay, of course. Don't you suppose he could be accommodated at Quimby's?"

Quimby's was the boarding-house patronized by Mr. Phillips. He had no doubt it could be done; whereupon Mr. Griggs turned over the new-comer to the care of his foreman, and resumed his work.

It was an extremely embarrassing position for Mr. Phillips. He never more fully felt his awkwardness. He stared at the stranger until the stranger looked up at him, and then he removed his eyes with a jerk. As speedily as possible he worked him over to the case, where, surrounded by the type and sticks, he found inspiration in the implements of his trade, and in a short time possessed himself of much information in regard to the recruit, and had struck up quite an acquaintance.

Mr. Griggs worked away very industriously for a half-hour longer; then he put on his cuffs and coat, straightened his hair, replaced his pipe with a cigar, donned his hat, and hurried away with a sigh of relief.

CHAPTER II.

THE EDITOR IN AN UNOFFICIAL LIGHT.

EDITOR GRIGGS walked rapidly after leaving the office of "The Gazette." The air was keen and crisp, and the hard-beaten snow creaked beneath his step. The stores were still in a blaze of light, and the walk was full of hurrying pedestrians, for it was yet early; but the editor paid no attention to any one or any thing. He hastened on, his eyes full of glad anticipation, and his cheeks aglow from the same emotion. At almost every stride he quickened his pace, and seemed to be trying to avoid recognition. On a street off from the main thoroughfare, he turned into the yard of a small, unpretentious house; ran up on the side-porch; opened its door, through whose curtained sash a light shone; and stepped into the sitting-room of the place, and almost directly into the arms of a young woman.

"O Tom!" she cried, as she clasped him around the neck, "what makes you so late?"

"I couldn't help it, Annie," he said, as he

turned a remarkably pretty face upward, and buried its lips in his mustache. "There was a chap came in to get a 'sit,'" he added, on resurrecting the lips, "and that kept me. And, by George! what a start he gave me! I thought he was a poet."

His voice sobered down so suddenly upon the utterance of this foreboding, that the young girl laughed outright. It was such a cheery, happy laugh, and showed to such advantage the tempting mouth that gave it voice, that the sexton was again pressed into service.

"O Tom! what a pest you are!" she cried, as soon as she was able. "I believe you will smother me some day."

As he turned the face up, so that his eyes and the light fell upon it, he looked very much as if he were two-thirds inclined to commit the awful deed on the spot. It was a bright, loving face; and, as Tom Griggs looked down upon it, he felt his heart swell with pride.

"Pet," he earnestly exclaimed, "you are the handsomest darling in all the world."

"Am I, Tom?" she whispered softly, her cheeks flushing with pleasure.

"Are you? Why, you know you are."

"I know I am to you, Tom; and that is enough." Then she drew the plump arms closer about his neck, and nestled her face on his shoulder.

The black hair, smooth and lustrous, was so

beautiful in his eyes, that he passed his hand over it again and again ; and, while he did so, he softly whispered, —

"My darling, my darling!"

And, under the caress and the whisper, the girl's heart swelled with pride, and her eyes filled with tears.

Happy woman! with his strong arm about her, his hand's touch thrilling her, his intense nature loving her, and his manly voice calling her the dearest names.

Happy man! with her woman's heart all his, the loving arms tight about him, the beautiful face radiant with love to *him*. It was all his, — the handsome features, the glossy hair, the shapely form, — all, all *his*. What a blessed inspiration it was to him! How his heart filled, his eyes brightened, his soul thrilled, under the impulse of the thought!

"Ah, Tom Griggs!" he involuntarily exclaimed, "if ever there was a fortunate man in all God's earth, *you* are the one."

The form in his arms quivered in an ecstasy of delight at this passionate utterance.

"My darling!" she murmured, nestling still closer to him.

. And Tom held her tight in both arms now, and kissed the beautiful hair, and forgot that he was the editor of a country newspaper, with the publication day close at hand. No other thought came into his mind but that of her; and no other thought, had he his way, should ever find entrance within the portals of his soul. He was not wearied to stand there : it was no burden to sustain her. Looking down upon the shapely head, feeling her faithful heart throbbing against his own, he fell to questioning whether it was not his duty to yield up his life at once in an ecstasy of delight as a sort of imperfect thank-offering.

"O Annie!" he cried, "if I never need go away from you again!"

"I know it, Tom," she murmured. "You come to me every night now; but yet the time between seems *so* long. Only a little while, and then we shall never be separated." She said this in her patient, hopeful, woman's way.

It did not seem possible that he could draw her any closer to himself than she was already ; but he did.

"Why, Tom," she cried, as soon as she could catch her breath, "you will surely kill me."

If pressure would kill, she certainly stood in imminent danger of passing hence under that process ; and there is no telling what might have been the result had not a step sounded on the porch. The door opened almost immediately, and a young girl entered the room. As quick as the lovers were in the movement produced by this entrance, they were not quick enough to blind her eyes to the probabilities.

"Why, Tom," she exclaimed, with a smile and a glance at both, "how long have you been here?"

It was noticeable of her face that the smile came suddenly, lighted her features in a flash, and then went again, leaving no trace of its presence. It was a grave, serious face in repose; but the smile made it radiant.

"About a minute," said the young man in answer, striving, in the rectitude of his nature, to be quite exact.

"Where's mother, Annie?" she asked of her sister.

"She's over to Quimby's. Mrs. Quimby has got a sore throat or something."

The young girl passed into another room to remove her wraps, an opportunity Mr. Griggs promptly economized by a use of the sexton.

"O Tom!" laughingly protested his betrothed.

The young girl, returning to the sitting-room, drew a rocker to the stove, and, seating herself, placed her feet to warm them, and rested her cheek on her hand. In this position she looked at the fire as if in a dream. It was a very serious face, — a tenderly sad face. She was not as handsome as her sister. Her features lacked the regularity and the full rich color; but their expression was so fraught with tenderness as to redeem the plainness. Perhaps this expression was but a reflection of her eyes. Soul-eyes they could be called, so full were they of light, — dark, deep blue eyes, luminous with purity. Not five out of every one hundred persons claiming blue eyes really possess them. There are but two positive

colors in eyes, — black and blue. The brown eye
is but an unsuccessful attempt to be black; the
gray eye is a futile endeavor to be blue; the hazel
eye is an unhappy reach after both.

"Where have you been, Lucy?" asked Tom,
after a few minutes' silence.

"I have been to the post-office. Did you come
direct here from your office?"

"Yes."

"It is odd I didn't see you," she said.

It may have been strange that she did not see
him on the way, but not at all strange that he
didn't see her. It is more than likely that he
would have climbed directly over her, without so
much as noticing her presence, in his eagerness to
reach her sister. However, he did not say so.

Shortly after, Lucy retired to the kitchen fire,
and the lovers were left to themselves.

Tom Griggs was coming every night to the
Bayard mansion. He and Annie were betrothed,
and in a few long (as contemplated) weeks they
were to be married. So Tom came every night;
and, often as it was, it was scarcely often enough.
The days were long and tedious to both of them;
and they were mostly consumed, we fear, in an-
ticipating and longing for the night. To these
two devoted souls the day which was to unite
them forever in this life was most eagerly yearned
after. If Editor Griggs, in his capacity as pub-
lisher, had been deputed to bring out an almanac,
it is reasonable to suppose that the volume would

be chiefly noted for the brevity of its contents before his wedding-day, and for their abundance ever after. Fortunately for the interests of the world at large, he was not thus deputed.

Mrs. Bayard had returned from a survey and a diagnosis of Mrs. Quimby's throat; Mr. Bayard had got back from, and lost all consciousness of, the church business-meeting; and Lucy had merged her waking dream into that of sleep, — when Tom Griggs' sexton had performed the last office for the night.

If our editor failed to hear the town-clock strike one, it was directly owing to his not getting out-doors in time. As he hurried along the deserted streets, he gave utterance to a sentiment having such a familiar sound as to seem almost like an echo from all the generations gone before, —

"What a donkey I was to stay so late! Here I've got to be up early in the morning, with a hard day's work before me, and I will feel like a fool to do it."

There *are* re-actions.

CHAPTER III.

MR. PHILLIPS BECOMES CONFIDENTIAL.

THE articles pertaining to Mr. Phillips' trade gave him confidence in himself. Being surrounded by objects familiar develops our self-reliance. They make ourselves seem more, and strangers less. A village young man, dressed in swell attire by the home tailor, passes through the familiar streets and by the familiar objects with a consciousness of his excellent appearance that he cannot help feeling. It is born of the circumstances. The garments fit him to a nicety. They cause him to be lifted up; they exalt him. There is nothing to depress the bump of self-esteem: on the contrary, there is every thing to develop it, and round it into a symmetrical sphere. He feels that he is "the observed of all observers." He experiences no embarrassment. He moves gracefully. Going into the city, he encounters a radical change. It amazes and depresses him. His clothes appear common; the fit execrable. Nobody gives them admiring attention. He feels awkward, out of place, uncomfortable. He is ill at ease, and is confident everybody is aware of it. He thought to mix with the city, and be of the city; but now he is as thoroughly known to be from the country as if he were placarded as such by a responsible house. It is a disheartening experience, but valuable if rightly heeded.

With the smell of the type and the ink ascending his nostrils, and the various articles of his trade filling his sight, Mr. Phillips immediately "felt at home," — a phrase expressing ease of manner. In a brief time he had satisfactorily explored the antecedents of Redner, and possessed himself of much valuable information. It was very comforting information, too, in that it showed him that the fund of printing knowledge carried around by the stranger was not sufficient to excite an alarm in his own breast of being superseded. The foreman of a country printing-office is a susceptible being, of strikingly apprehensive tendencies.

In return for the information extracted from the new journeyman, Mr. Phillips acquainted him with various essential facts, including the circulation of "The Gazette;" the length of time he had been there; his ability as a printer; Mr. Griggs' dependence upon him; the uplifted condition of the entire office now, as compared to what it was when he took charge; with a summary of the demands of the trade, and the inability of other printers, with scarcely an exception, to cope with them.

Having contributed these well-digested bits of information for the edification of his companion, he said that they might as well be getting toward

Quimby's, which the other favoring, they departed. On their way through the main street, Mr. Phillips kindly pointed out the various business-places, tersely indicating their standing by the degree of their advertising. The parties who did not advertise at all, he properly ignored. He pointed out the post-office, the banks, two new buildings, the place where there had been a fire four months before, — "an old he-one," to use Mr. Phillips's chaste imagery, — and other objects of absorbing interest. Before one building, larger than the others, he suddenly stopped.

"This is the hotel," he explained. "Do you ever take any thing?" There was a shade of anxiety in his voice.

His companion said he did not.

"I'm not in favor of drinking myself," hastily confessed Mr. Phillips (people who drink rarely are); "but once in a while I believe a little liquor does a man good, especially after he's been to work as I have to-day. They've got the best cider-brandy here you ever set your eyes on."

Mr. Phillips, having delivered this bit of suggestive information, looked anxiously into the face of his companion.

"I don't think I want any to-night, thank you," said the young man. "Can you get pie there?"

"Pie? Oh, yes!"

"Well, I'll take a piece of pie, then," ventured the young man. ·

This offer struck Mr. Phillips so favorably, that

he at once fell in with it ; and, stepping into the bar of the building, he ordered a glass of cider-brandy for himself, and a quarter of pie for the other, and then, with a nod to the stranger, and the intelligible and complimentary observation, " Here's to you ! " decorously tipped the contents of the glass down his throat. Having thus strengthened himself, and provided for the future welfare of his new acquaintance, he paid for the articles, and they returned to the street.

" I can tell you, Redner, that's the stuff ! " he confidentially observed, as they moved along. " If a man never drank any thing but liquor like that, there would be mighty few drunkards, I can tell you." This statement struck Mr. Phillips so favorably, that he repeated it twice with unction. Then he branched off on other topics, which, being taken on a cider-brandy basis, were handled most elaborately.

Proceeding through a side-street, Mr. Phillips pointed to a house across the way, and said, —

" Griggs' girl lives there."

" Is that so ? " said Redner. " Is she handsome ? "

" She's a buster," pronounced Mr. Phillips with great feeling.

His companion looked puzzled.

" She can just lap over any girl in these parts, and don't you forget it," said Mr. Phillips strongly. " I have seen women in my time, — lots of 'em ; but I never saw the woman that could hold a

candle to her. When you lay your eyes on *her*"
(here Mr. Phillips took Redner impressively by
the arm), "it will rest 'em."

"Then she is very handsome?" said the other
in a tone of deep interest.

"You can bet your bottom dollar on it," affirmed Mr. Phillips. "You ought to see her
eyes— By Judas! if she ain't got the blackest
eyes you ever saw! Not hard black eyes, you
know, but a kind of a soft black, as if they were
going to melt, and run all over her." Mr. Phillips
sighed heavily at this reflection; but whether from
a vividness of the delicious picture he had con-
jured up, or from a contemplation of the waste
suggested in the running over, he did not explain.

"You were saying"— put in Redner with
heightened interest.

"Oh, yes!" continued Mr. Phillips. "But
there's no use trying to do justice to that girl's
eyes. When she puts 'em on you, you feel just
like crawling under the mud out of sight. It
makes a man think he is less than nothing, and
willing to swear to it. And then her cheeks!—
oh, my!" Mr. Phillips smacked his lips, and smote
his hands in an ecstasy of feeling.

"Are they rosy?" interrupted Redner.

"Rosy!" exclaimed Mr. Phillips in some dis-
dain. "Humph! That ain't no name for it.
There's not another such a pair of cheeks in all
Gallowhill. They make me think of a water-
melon every time I see 'em."

His companion looked aghast. But Mr. Phillips did not notice it. He said, —

"You have seen these awful dead-ripe water-melons, ain't you, that are so red that they look white — a sort of powdered white — on the edges?"

Redner nodded.

"Well, her cheeks are just like that." Mr. Phillips sighed again, and looked a shade more solemn than before. At this juncture he turned into a gateway, observing, —

"This is Quimby's."

Without the ceremony of knocking, he passed into the house; and, leaving Redner in a small sitting-room, he went in search of Mrs. Quimby. In a moment or so he returned, accompanied by a heavily built lady with a very red face, and a throat swathed in flannel. A delicate odor of arnica hovered about her. Mr. Phillips introduced her as Mrs. Quimby. She told Redner, in a slightly masculine voice, that he was welcome, and said he must pardon her appearance, as she was suffering from an attack of sore throat.

"It's an old enemy of mine, and gives me a sight of trouble," she explained. "I do every thing for it, and try every thing, and have had the doctors fuss with it; but nothing does any good. It is there; an' it's likely it'll stay there as long as I'm alive. No one can tell what I suffer from it; for I don't believe in making a great hue-an'-cry over myself. But, if ninety-nine out of a hundred women had my complaint, they'd never think of

getting out of bed. But I keep up an' moving
around. It's only my ambition that keeps me up,
though. If it wa'n't for that, I'd go down in a
heap many a time. But what's the use of giving
up, an' going to bed? It's all folly. People say
to me, 'Why, Mrs. Quimby, how *do* you keep up
so? I should think you'd be abed a-doctorin' yourself,' says they. 'But what's the use?' I tell 'em.
'If I went to bed, I'd just tumble around, an' think
of the work; an' it wouldn't do me a bit of good.'
No, indeed: work it off, is my motto; an' work it
off I do. No one hears me complain; for I don't
believe in whining an' grumbling: they never did
any good; they only make things worse. No one
hears me doing it: do they, Mr. Phillips?"

Mr. Phillips started like one suddenly awakened
from a drowse, and unhappily said, "Yes, indeed!"

"Why, Mr. Phillips! when do I ever complain?" demanded the amazed and grieved lady.

Mr. Phillips, being now thoroughly awake,
hastily explained that he was so engrossed in
thinking of a programme in two colors which he
had to get out the next day, that he was afraid he
might not have perfectly heard her question.
Mrs. Quimby repeated it. Then Mr. Phillips
promptly said, —

"I guess you don't."

This point being satisfactorily settled, and it
further transpiring, as admitted by himself, that
Mr. Redner never had had any throat-trouble,
the terms of board were agreed upon. Mrs.

Quimby was sorry she could not give him a room to himself at present; and he would have to share Mr. Phillips' room, which that gentleman kindly offered, and which, having a fire, would be, on the whole, quite as agreeable. The new boarder being satisfied with this arrangement, he was escorted by Mr. Phillips to the room.

It was a very good-sized apartment, and contained, in addition to a bed, a cot, which Mr. Phillips indicated to his company that he was to occupy. He further showed him the closet for his clothes, the wash-stand, &c., and then withdrew for a few minutes. During his absence Redner unpacked his valise, and arranged his articles of apparel for the occupancy of the room. Several volumes of novels and a story-paper were among his effects. Of these he appeared to be very choice; and, after he got through with the valise, he took a seat by the fire, opened the paper, and became at once absorbed in its contents. When Mr. Phillips returned, he found him thus engaged.

"What's that you're reading?"

"A story. Do you ever read romances, Mr. Phillips?"

"Not many. When I was a boy I didn't do much of any thing else; but I don't have time for that business now."

"How old is Annie Bayard?"

"About twenty, I should say," replied Mr. Phillips, taking off his coat and hat, and drawing a chair up to the fire. "By jinks! this is comfort, ain't it?" he added, with an air of satisfaction, as he spread his palms to the heat.

"Yes: it is cosey," indorsed Redner. "How long has Mr. Griggs kept company with Miss Bayard?"

"About a year, I think, though it may be longer. It's curious what a difference there is sometimes in people in one family. Annie has got a sister that don't look any more like her than — than"— Here Mr. Phillips looked around in some desperation for an object of comparison. "Well, than I do," he finally gasped.

His companion at once judged there were points of difference between the two sisters that could not very well be ignored.

"Is she much older?" he asked.

"No: she ain't so old by a year or thereabouts. I shouldn't think Lucy was much over eighteen."

"What kind of a young lady is she?"

"She's a mouse."

"What do you mean by that?" hastily demanded Redner.

"Why, that she's so quiet. You know they say, 'quiet as a mouse,' although I can't say that *I* ever noticed any thing particularly quiet about a mouse. She's the stillest girl I ever saw. She don't go into company much, and is rather pious. Do you ever go around among women much?"

"Some."

Mr. Phillips was silent a moment, watching the smoke from his pipe. Then he bent his eyes earnestly on Redner, and asked, —

"Were you ever in love?"

"I? No."

"Don't you like women at all?"

"Oh, yes! I am a great admirer of ladies. But I am not in love with any particular one."

"Don't you think," asked Mr. Phillips, after another pause, "that woman is a flattener?"

"A flattener?" repeated Redner, opening his eyes in astonishment.

"Why, yes; that is, don't you think she is a knock-over sort of thing?"

The young man's face not expressing a clear comprehension of this, Mr. Phillips was obliged to be more exact.

"What I mean is, that she's a settler,—kinder knocks the life out of you, you know."

Redner was obliged to confess that he had never felt compelled to view the sex in that light.

"But it is so," affirmed Mr. Phillips gloomily; "and, when you've had experience with 'em, you will know it for a fact. I have been there, and I know. I might have been married twice over before now, if it wa'n't for that." At this juncture Mr. Phillips fell back on the pipe, smoking rapidly.

"You have been in love, then?" Redner ventured to inquire, after a moment's silence.

"I suppose it can be called that," whiffed Mr. Phillips.

"Was the lady— was the lady averse to the offer?"

It was a delicate question, and hesitatingly propounded.

"I never found out," gloomily replied Mr. Phillips.

"How was that?"

"Because woman is a flattener," was the short reply.

"I am afraid I do not understand you," said Redner.

"It is easy enough to understand if you had been there," answered Mr. Phillips, refilling his pipe. "A woman is all right when looked at, like a jack-knife or a saw-mill or a panorama; but when you get fastened to her, when you get all twisted up in her, when your heart and mind is all in a condemned tangle and snarl,— then she is an altogether different object; then she becomes a flattener, a keel-overer. When you go to say any thing to her, you can't do it; and, for all you know about what's what, you might as well be standing on your muddled head in the middle of Patagonia. Yes, sir, I might have been married twice over, if it wa'n't for that; but my blamed stomach comes back on me every time." Mr. Phillips' face had been lowering all the while he was speaking, and at this juncture the ferocity of its expression was really alarming. "Yes, sir, every time," he continued, smiting his knee. "I get along all right until I come to the sticking-point, and then I flop ker-chunk. My blamed stomach comes back on me, and I fizzle out like a busted bladder." The foreman of "The Gazette" pulled vigorously at his pipe for a moment. "I have such a sinking right here," placing his hand on his abdomen, and sighing solemnly, "as if my palate, loaded with old iron, had dropped there. · I can't tell how it is ; but there is such an awful goneness right in the pit of my stomach, that it takes away my breath as clean as if it was whipped out of me by the kick of a mule."

After this explanation, Mr. Phillips moodily pulled away at the pipe ; while his companion, feeling perhaps that the sorrow was far beyond the reach of sympathy, offered no comment.

It was some ten minutes before the silence was broken. Mr. Phillips emptied his pipe, and announced he would go to bed, — a purpose he immediately put into execution. Redner also retired, but not to sleep. He lay in his bed, looking at the moving shadows as formed by the flickering light from the stove, and pondering on woman as revealed to him in the new and somewhat startling character of "a flattener."

CHAPTER IV.

PUBLICATION DAY.

UNDER the convoy of the estimable Mr. Phillips, the stranger reached the office of "The Gazette" and the field of his labor shortly after seven o'clock the next morning. The foreman, being entirely free of all trace of the influence of flattening, was wholly absorbed in the duties of the day. He gave Redner a case, and piece of reprint from a county paper for copy, and introduced him to a middle-aged man, of consumptive aspect, who had a case at his side. This party had a thin, reddish beard, and a very white face, and looked as if he had been composed of the ingredients of a printing-office, so thoroughly did he seem to partake of the nature of the metal and ink and oil and paper around him. Redner saw that the other employees were a young man of about his own age, who appeared dissipated, and a boy of some fifteen summers, who, early as it was in the day, had got a pretty smart sprinkling of ink on his hands and face. Redner noticed, that, whenever he looked toward these two, they were in the very act of taking their gaze from him. He did not know that they had heard already that he was from the great city of Boston, or that a city youth possesses a peculiar charm to a village youth. At his case he could command a view of the door and the sanctum. Mr. Griggs had not yet arrived; but his desk was not quite idle, as Mr. Phillips was frequently there getting copy, and looking into letters and other papers. All the proceedings of the business had an attraction to Redner. It was his first experience in a country printing-office. He was surprised at the familiarity existing on the part of the employees toward the foreman, which did not appear to be heartily reciprocated by him. Even the "devil" called him Ez. He noticed, also, the familiarity of the employees with the office itself and the office terms. So conspicuous was this, that he could not help noticing it. In their use of the terms, it was charming to note the carelessness of the utterance, as if these expressions were common, every-day matters, and not brought out for the occasion. Strangers visiting a printing-office are startled by the flippancy with which the "hell-box" is referred to, the "devil" inquired after, and the "dead" disposed of. There is that to knowledge which makes it a delight to air itself, unless there is a great deal of it.

In addition to all, it seemed to fall upon the sandy-bearded man to be captious, the youth of twenty to be indifferent, and the boy with the inked features to be impudent; and on all a spirit of remark upon contributors and advertisers that

was certainly conspicuous for breadth and freedom.
The dissipated youth and the "devil" said "naw"
when answering in the negative, and "damn" frequently, and were much addicted to a short, scorn-
ful laugh.   All their profanity, like their slang,
was delivered with a peculiar unction.   These
two showed a disposition to appear ten years older
than they really were, and quite often made a
painful exhibition of the effort.   Redner learned
that the sandy-whiskered man was named Hazelton; the dissipated youth, Joe Goodwin; and the
boy, Henry Vanderlip, — which name had been
happily brought down to "Lippy" by the office.
All smoked and chewed.

About eight o'clock Mr. Griggs appeared, and
briskly took position at the desk, although his
eyes had any thing but a wide-awake expression.
Ezekiah was immediately in consultation with
him, and frequently thereafter.   These consulta-
tions appeared to consist, on the part of Mr.
Griggs, in assertion, and on the part of Mr. Phillips in protestation, and referred mainly to an endeavor on the part of the former to squeeze two
columns of copy into one column of space.   Mr.
Phillips acted as the representative of space, and
maintained a gallant, although not always successful, fight in its behalf.   Redner noticed, as the day
advanced, that Ezekiah became more wary, yet
agressive, while, Mr. Griggs grew correspondingly
timid and propitiatory, even handing out the copy
toward the last in an apologetic manner.   The new
journeyman wondered very much at this.

Every few minutes through the day he saw the door open, and some one appear. These embraced a variety of people. Early in the hour they seemed to consist mostly of slim persons, neatly dressed, and of a bustling air, who dealt directly with the proprietor, and who appeared to be advertisers, judging from their remarks. He further noticed that those of this lot who came the latest had the longest advertisements to insert, and that their favors were not new notices, but changes of those already in. These men had a great deal to say, and appeared much surprised by what they heard, and caused Mr. Griggs much anxiety. It was also noticeable that the very prominent face of Mr. Phillips gave increased evidence of disgust at every one of these calls, and that it presented to the occasionally appealing glances of Editor Griggs a most uncompromising aspect. So greatly were Mr. Phillips' feelings worked upon by these advents, that every little while he would retire behind one of the racks, and, after a profane tussle with an imaginary adversary, would re-appear, apparently very much strengthened thereby, and more defiant than before.

Two or three of the visitors appeared to have so little object, that their aimlessness was as much a part of them as their clothes. They slouched in hesitatingly, looked about furtively, dealt in forced smiles, and suggested to Redner that they had been created without special reference to their use, but in the rather vague hope that they would

some time prove available for "filling in." They
may have come in to learn if the paper was out,
as each one asked the question; but, as they did
not go on being informed, that could not have
been the real object. They moved about the
room, looking at the forms; standing by the compositors, with whom they seemed acquainted; ask-
ing harmless questions; picking up articles of the
trade, and closely scrutinizing them; and picking
up newspapers or bills which they saw on the floor
or stands, and listlessly looking at them. Each
one of these staid an hour or so, got thoroughly
warmed, and as much in the way as possible, and
then drifted out doors.

Occasionally an elderly gentleman would come
in, and taking out his glasses and wiping them,
and attending to his nose, and dusting off a chair,
would seat himself; performing all these acts in a
methodical manner, that, while it was not exactly
exciting, certainly possessed a peculiar fascination
to the observer. On settling himself, and learning
that the paper was not printed, the elderly gentleman would peer anxiously among the exchanges;
make a few suggestions of a valuable, but somewhat intricate, nature; inquire who had written
some certain article that had appeared the week
before, if so-and-so had any thing in the coming
paper; and then, removing his glasses and restor-
ing them, and again attending to his nose, would
say he didn't know what the poor were going to
do this winter; and finally depart, leaving the
door unlatched.

By far the largest number of visitors as to class were those who came merely to inquire if the paper was out. Redner was surprised at the size of this multitude; and had he not had a verbal statement of the circulation of "The Gazette," and the pile of paper ready for the press before him, would have readily believed that the number of copies printed was fully eight times greater than it really was. There was considerable variety to this number, both in their appearance and conduct. The greater part were horny-handed and heavily bearded men, who were muffled heavily about the neck, and stepped heavily. They evidently lived in the outer districts, and would like to take the paper home with them; they appeared somewhat disappointed in not finding the paper ready, and seemed inclined to stand by the stove, and stare about the room, but particularly at the type-setters. Of the others, many made comments of a derogatory or facetious or sarcastic nature, calculated to reflect on the character of the office in the matter of promptness.

There was another lot, who appeared to have something they wanted published in the present issue; and Editor Griggs was obliged to devote one-third of his time in expostulating with, or explaining to, or smoothing down, these clients.

Redner noticed, that, as the hours advanced, his employer's nervousness increased; that his face became flushed, his movements jerky and uncertain, and his tones peevish. In the proof-reading he would frequently launch an execration at the head of one of the compositors, and the victim would respond in an injured tone that was audible, and in another tone that was not so.

Mr. Phillips himself was not less affected than his superior.   His temper, which was none too good at the start, had become so sore and inflamed as to fill Redner with the liveliest apprehension of the result.   He appeared to look upon every visitor who gave any indication of having manuscript on his person as an unprincipled scoundrel, who was working in an underhand way for the destruction of the establishment, and felt it to be his sacred duty to scowl at him with a degree of ferocity that was beyond describing.

At the last hour, nearly all the spare space of the office was filled with anxious persons, who watched every movement with so much intentness as to be very gratifying to the bustling Mr. Phillips, who, having the forms of the paper so far advanced as to effectually shut out the introduction of more copy, was relieved of a great incubus, and had only to take care of and exhibit the dignity of his position to the best advantage.   It was really a delight to watch him, observing the swiftness of his movements, and the splurge of his manner; while to see him cuff the "devil" on the side of the head, or fling a quoin — which either did not fit or was broken — across the room, was a most enjoyable sensation.

Finally, the forms were made ready, and put on

the press ; the "devil " took his place at the distributor ; and the press started. As fast as copies were turned out, the waiting readers seized them, until all were supplied. Redner was directed to fold, in which occupation he had the improving companionship of the dissipated youth. Occasionally the dissipated youth would relieve Mr. Phillips at the press. It was nearly ten o'clock at night when the last paper was worked off, and the "devil" was then in a state of ink, from his heel to his crown, that was simply amazing.

Mr. Griggs had gone away at nine o'clock,— "to Bayard's," Mr. Phillips whispered ; and the hands were left to attend to the papers that were to go by mail the next morning. At eleven o'clock Redner and the foreman started home ; the latter stopping at the hotel to " brace up," and the former taking a piece of pie, of which he appeared to be quite fond. Before midnight the young man was abed, and dreaming that a roll of manuscript had come into the office of " The Gazette," and that Mr. Phillips had brained it with the shooting-stick at the very threshold of the door.

CHAPTER V.

AT THE PRAYER-MEETING.

THE new journeyman, on the following evening, finding a discussion on liquor-drinking between Mr. Quimby and Mr. Phillips did not interest him, left those two worthies thus engaged in the little back sitting-room of his boarding-house, and took a stroll through the village, to make himself acquainted with some of its features. It was a clear, bright night; and Redner, walking through the crisp air, divided his time on Main Street between the stars and the ladies he chanced to encounter. He walked leisurely, the restless expression of his eyes somewhat modified. He followed Main Street nearly the length of its business-section, but showed little or no interest in the stores. Many of them had dingy fronts, of small glass, dimly lighted by kerosene-lamps; as gas in Gallowhill was five dollars a thousand, and the country merchants found it necessary to economize. But, listlessly as he moved, he could not avoid noticing that the fronts of the hardware-stores showed less light than any of the others, and that the inside of the doors was hung with whips and sleigh-bells and chains. Beyond this he showed no interest in the places of business, but walked along, looking intently into the faces of the females he met. Crossing a street that intersected Main Street, he heard a church-bell ring. He looked up the street whence the sound came, but saw no light to indicate the presence of the building. For a moment he paused irresolutely, as if debating a point, and then he abruptly turned in an opposite direction. The starlight and the snowlight showed him that he was on a street of private houses, with capacious front-yards, darkened by sombre evergreens. He walked in this direction for some little distance, but, encountering nobody, turned about, and retraced his way. On returning to Main Street, he recalled the tolling bell, and, after a moment's pause, went up the street leading to it.

A moment of quick stepping brought him to the church. There was an open door leading into the porch of the basement. He went in there, and listened a moment to the sounds coming from the room beyond. Some one was either talking or praying. As the voice ceased, he passed into the room, and found himself in a prayer-meeting.

There was no difficulty in securing a seat. A very fair-sized battalion of troops could have been accommodated without seriously crowding the congregation. It was not a particularly attractive room, although Redner's restless eyes kept upon the people, and failed to notice this. The ceiling

was low, and the plaster cracked and stained.
The walls were relieved here and there from the
monotony of color by a biblical map or a scriptu-
ral text, the nature of which showed that the
apartment was used for Sunday-school purposes
also.   The floor was covered with well-worn mat-
ting; the sittings were settees without cushions;
a large stove stood in the middle of the room; a
dozen or so of posts sustained the floor above, and
served to screen as many timid brethren from
range of the leader's vision.   This person was a
short, stout man, with a sandy beard, light-colored
eyes, and a very austere shirt-collar.   His chair
was on a raised platform, back of a small table.
The room was capable of seating three hundred
persons.   About one-tenth of that number were
present.   A majority of these were females, and
the greater part of all were of middle age and
beyond.   There were three little folks present, —
two girls and a boy.   The little girls were very
prim; and the little boy appeared to be nearly, if
not wholly, petrified.   The room was scarcely more
sombre than the people, and each seemed to be in
keeping with the other.   It was the temple of the
Lord of the universe; and these were his people
come to rejoice and be glad in his presence, without doubt.

Nearly every eye was turned on Redner when
he entered, and many glances were cast toward
him during the service.   As he took a seat, the
leader gave out a hymn.   It was a heavy hymn

with a heavy air, and seemed to require that the
voices should get way down under it to lift it up,
and set it going all right. After this labor was
performed, and the gloom of the apartment appeared to densify under its pulsation, the leader
observed, with fixed solemnity, —

"We have come together, brethren and sisters,
for the purpose of conference and prayer. This is
one of the most blessed privileges vouchsafed us
in our religious life; and we should come with our
offerings, rejoicing that we have the opportunity
to contribute in so good a cause. I hope to-night
that there will be no delays, but that each one
will be ready with a word of testimony for the
Lord, taking up his cross promptly and cheerfully,
and so making it an active, pleasant, and profitable
service. Don't let there be any waiting one for
another, but all pray or speak as they see fit."

There was an oppressive pause of a full moment's duration after this, during which the leader
looked stonily ahead, as if he had fully discharged
his duty in the matter, and was relieved of all
responsibility for the consequences. And then
he said, "Brother Mercer, will you lead us in
prayer?"

In response to this request, a large man with
very little hair on his head laboriously rose,
clasped his hands reverently across his stomach,
and, closing his eyes heavily, proceeded, in a se-
pulchral voice, to spread out his views before the
Almighty. The voice being not at all natural,

although adapted, without doubt, to a public
prayer, required considerable effort to keep it up
to the mark. For five minutes he rumbled on,
growing more grandly elaborate in the progress,
and finally rounded off with a sonorous "Amen."

Another pause followed, in which Brother Mercer mopped off the top of his head, and looked
around upon the stolid faces about him as if to
say, "I think *that* covered the ground in a very
handsome manner."

"Don't let the time go to waste, brethren,"
urged the leader, looking over the congregation
so briskly as to cause the brethren back of the
posts to contract themselves to a degree that was
painful.

Another large man rose. The parties back of
the posts sighed and expanded. The large man
cleared his throat, — an act imposed by his standing up, undoubtedly, — and, looking fixedly over
the heads of the assembly, sternly observed, —

"Brethren and sisters, it is a blessed privilege
to stand up and testify for the Master. [Throat.]
He has done every thing for us. [Throat.] And
we should be willing to do every thing for him.
[Throat.] To speak for him, and to tell the joy
[throat] we feel in serving him, is a duty we owe
him. [Throat.] This is a service, a blessed service, that none of us should try to shirk. [Throat.]
As for myself, I feel that the Lord has been very
good to me. [Throat.] And I want to serve him
better than I do. [Throat.] We all make crooked

paths for our feet, and wander away [throat] from the strait and narrow path, which is not right." [Three throats.]

This encouraging summary of the general spiritual condition emboldened a tall, thin man, with whiskers under his chin, to get up, and heartily indorse the sentiment by cheerfully announcing, —

"I don't feel as if I am in the right way, brethren and sisters. I do, as the brother has said, make many crooked paths for my feet, and wander in by and forbidden ways. I am growing cold and indifferent; but, if I know my own heart, I know that I want to be a better Christian: I want to be willing to take up my cross in these meetings, and testify of His goodness to me. It is a joy to tell of Jesus' wonderful goodness. Let us all take up our cross, and be more active. Pray for me, brethren and sisters, that I may be more faithful."

He sat down with a sigh, and an oppressive pause followed.

"Now, let's hear from another," said the leader briskly. "I know it is a hard cross to get up and speak a word for our Saviour; but, if we are determined to do it, we will find the effort to be easier and easier. Let us sing one verse of 'Am I a Soldier of the Cross?' and then let some one follow right after in prayer or exhortation."

The verse was sung with due solemnity, and another painful pause succeeded, causing the zealous disciples back of the posts to contract within their respective spheres as much as possible.

"Don't let the time go to waste," besought the leader.

An old man rose.

"I don't want to take up valuable time, and deprive others of speaking," was his ghastly announcement; "but I am always glad to have an opportunity to speak a word for my Saviour. I have been forty years in this service, and I find it is a blessed service to engage in. I have done many things in that time which I hadn't oughter done, and I have left undone many things that I had oughter done. I hope none of you won't take me for an example of what to do, but do your full duty at all times and everywhere. There's nothing like living close up to the mark in the Christian life. The flesh is weak, as we've been told; but we have One which can help us, who has been tried as we are, and knows just what we want, and will give it to us if we will only go to Him, and ask Him to help us. Let us try to be more faithful, brethren and sisters; let us try to work more in His vineyard. The work is easy, and the pay is sure. Pray for me, that I may ever be found faithful and willing to take up my cross."

After him and another very oppressive pause, in which the disciples back of the posts threatened to shrink into mere wads of cloth, a thin young man laboriously observed, —

"I love Jesus, and want to take up my cross, and follow him. If there is any one here who hasn't come to Christ, I would say, Come to-night, and take up your cross, and follow him."

Then he sat down; and the leader, after a moment's waiting, asked, —

"Isn't there another that has got one word to speak for the Saviour. He bore the cross for us. Can we not bear the cross for him? Just one word." Here his eyes roamed over the audience, to the great discomfort of some, without doubt. "Brother Reynolds," he pleasantly called, as his glance rested upon a sandy-haired man, and a winning smile illuminated his face, "shall we not have a word from you this evening?"

Brother Reynolds's very white face became very red as this mark of distinction smote him. He struggled to his feet, and clung convulsively to the back of the seat in front of him, —

"I— I— I am glad of the oppor— opportunity to take up my cross," he gratefully gasped, "and — and— and I hope I— you— I may be found on the-e-e-e side"— Here his voice nearly died away; but by a powerful effort he dove down, and brought it up: "Pray for me that I may be always— that I may take up my cross. And"— He paused, with a gurgling noise in his throat, as if catching after his treacherous breath. "Pray for me," he despairingly gasped, "that I may take up my cross." At this juncture his voice fell through again, and he straightway plunged after it, half secured it, lost it, and dropped heavily into his seat; and immediately drew out a large handkerchief, with which he mopped great drops of perspiration from his face.

Another verse was sung at the request of the leader.

"The time is arrived for closing," he said ; "but there may be some one who would like to speak a word, and we will wait a moment longer. I do not want to deprive any one of the opportunity of bearing the cross. It is blessed duty, brethren and sisters. Is there not another? We will wait a minute."

He paused, and looked inquiringly around the room.

There was the rustle of a dress, and a young woman rose. She had her back toward Redner, so he could not see her face; but her form was graceful, and the mass of hair that fell from beneath the fleecy hood she wore was very beautiful. The expression of lassitude that had settled upon his countenance gave way immediately to a look of lively interest, and he opened his ears to hear what she would say. Her voice was low, but distinct and musical.

"I do not feel as if I can go from here," she said, "without saying something for my dear Saviour. His precious love has filled my heart all this day ; and I feel so happy in him, — far happier than I can tell. I thank him that he loves me, that he cares for me so constantly; but I thank him above all for his precious nearness to me in every hour of my life. Prayer is dear to me, and his word is a sweet comfort to me. I can say with all my heart, 'The Lord is my shepherd;' and, as I say it, I know that 'I shall not want.'"

That was all she said; but it interested Redner more than all the rest had said put together, and the room itself seemed to grow brighter as she said it.

Another hymn was sung, and the audience then dismissed. As Redner stood in his place to wait for her to pass out, he saw his employer in the doorway; and, as his glance fell on him, he observed his eyes light up, and saw him step quickly into the room, his face in a glow of delight, and become almost immediately blended with a happy-faced girl, whose own eyes fairly danced with glad expectation. Happy Tom Griggs! How his face shone! Redner could see him quiver all over as his hands tenderly adjusted her furs; and the beautiful face that was turned to his was but a reflex of his own happiness. The new journey-man watched them walk away, saw her snug so tightly up to him, saw him bend so lovingly over her, and then he knew that this was Anna Bayard.

When he had recovered himself, the girl whose words had so deeply impressed him was passing. In the same instant their eyes met. His gaze was bent on her with such fervency, that her eyes dropped at once, and her face flushed. She passed out of the building with an elderly man and woman, whom Redner surmised to be her parents. He immediately followed after them through several streets, until he saw them disappear within a house ; and standing opposite, and looking hard at the premises, he recollected that it was the house that Phillips had pointed out to him the night of his arrival as the home of the Bayards.

CHAPTER VI.

THE PICTURE OF A HAPPY FUTURE.

It was two o'clock A.M., as usual, when Tom Griggs got away from the Bayard mansion the night of the prayer-meeting.

"It does beat the devil" (the "devil" is the youngest apprentice in a printing-office), he mused to himself, as he hastened through the deserted streets, "that I haven't got the strength of mind to leave at a decent hour. Here it is near morning, and I out of bed, and a hard day's work before me! I'll feel like a fool in the morning, and it will be like pulling teeth to get me up. But what *am I* to do?" he added despairingly. "I swear every time I leave that the next night I will go home at ten o'clock; but, when ten o'clock comes, it seems as if I had only been there a minute, and I *can't* go away. Dear, precious Anna! God bless you! In a few days I shall have you always to myself, and then there will be no separating at night." He had lapsed into a slow pace as these softening thoughts came to him; but, suddenly rousing himself, he started rapidly forward. "There's no use talking! I *must* get away earlier than this. It won't do: the loss of sleep is killing me and my darling." How quickly the determined expression on his face melted away as he pronounced the loving title! "God bless her!" he softly murmured. "It won't be long now, and afterward we can rest out. I can't go earlier, there's so much to talk about; and she is so terribly dear to me. Would to heaven I never had to leave her for a single moment!"

Tom Griggs' face was less earnest than his legs as he hurried on. He entered his home, found the light as left for him by his thoughtful mother; and, after a call at the pantry, he retired to the icy embrace of his couch, to fight the chill, and to dream of Anna Bayard and the grand future opening its endless avenue of joy before them.

It didn't seem as if he had been fifteen minutes in bed — scarcely long enough to get to sleep, at any rate — when he was called to breakfast, and awoke to see the daylight filling his room.

It was a hard day's work that Tom had before him, and he was sorely tempted to murmur against the fate which doomed him to labor for his daily bread. He shivered as he hurried through the streets; and, when he reached the office, it was patent to the "devil" even that he had been up late. With all the discomfort of his indiscretion upon him, the editor of "The Gazette" declared over and over again that he would be more moderate the next time; and we are charitable enough to believe he meant it.

But, when Tom Griggs' day's work was done, the impatience he displayed in eating his supper, —which, it must be said, however inelegant it may sound, he fairly bolted, —and in getting his Sunday suit on, boded no good to the new resolve. He even cursed the hard-trodden snow on the walks, whose smooth surface prevented his feet from keeping pace with his desires, as he hastened on his way to the home of the Bayards. Nearly fifteen hours had passed since he had seen her. It was such a dreary, long time. It was like coming into sight of land after weeks of tempestuous ocean-voyaging, to come in sight of her home. He blessed the white paint and the green blinds, and the dead honeysuckle-vine swaying from the pillars of the porch. He called the house the casket which contained his jewel; and to him there was no fairy palace to equal it in magnificence. Fortunately he was not in quest of real estate, or he would have beggared himself and his friends to have obtained the location. The cosey sitting-room was just as we saw it on the first evening we followed Tom to the side of his promised bride. Anna was there, radiant with a welcoming smile. The rest of the family were in the dining-room, as indicated by the sound of the voices. What a sacred place was that dining-room to Tom Griggs! Several times he had taken tea there, and twice on Sundays (memorable occasions!) he had eaten dinner therein.

There is a desire born in the heart of every

young man to see her who is dearer than life to
him eat.   There is nothing unworthy in this.   It
is not to measure her capacity, or to observe how
graceful she is at such a time.   But it gives him a
nearness to her that is not otherwise obtained.   It
is typical of their own home : it is the foreshadow-
ing of the time when they shall be independent of
all others, and be left to lean alone upon each
other.   It made Tom Griggs feel as if he and
Anna were really a part of each other.

Tom was very happy as he took her lovingly
into his arms ; and he felt so thoroughly wide
awake and fresh, that it would be a sin to doubt
his ability to sit up all night if an emergency
should require, — not a very large emergency,
either.

And the dear girl who rested so fondly and
contentedly upon his breast forgot that she had
devoted the greater part of the day to keeping her
eyes open, even with the encouragement of seeing stitch after stitch forming order out of chaos
in a pile of fabrics before her.

This very same pile of sewing, the editor of
"The Gazette" saw at the machine ; and, while a
roguish light played in his eyes, he gravely inquired, —

"What's here, Anna?" and made as if he would
thoroughly investigate.

"Now, Tom, don't tease!" she cried, endeavor-
ing to hold him back, and blushing and laughing
in a most tantalizing way.

It must have been an inspiration that seized him, he took her up so suddenly and impetuously in his arms, and held her so tightly. ,.

"O Tom!" she gasped as soon as he freed her, "don't you know that the folks will hear you?"

"I don't care if they do," he boldly asserted. "Don't you suppose I've got the right to squeeze you, you beautiful witch?" And, before the unfortunate girl could save herself, he had her again in his impetuous embrace.

"Oo-oo! doon't — doo-ent!" she gasped. "O Tom!" after she got her breath, "I won't have a lung to breathe with."

"What!" exclaimed the young man in great surprise. "Do you call that squeezing? Wait till we are married, darling, and then you will call this child's play. I'll have you all to myself then, and there won't be any one around to interfere."

"I won't live with you then. I'll get a divorce, and come back home," she retorted laughingly, while her eyes shone with the love that filled her life.

He was going to make another pass for her, when her father appeared; and her lover's face assumed immediately an expression of such profound gravity, that the happy girl laughed outright.

"Good-evening, Mr. Bayard," said Tom.

"Good-evening, Tom," responded that gentleman, looking inquiringly at his daughter. "How's the weather out?"

Had the old gentleman devoted three entire

days to the construction of a most intricate problem, he could not have more completely floored
Tom than by this simple inquiry. In his haste to
reach his Anna, the young man had taken no note
of the weather, and for the life of him could give
no reliable data.

"Pretty cold, ain't it?" added the old gentleman helpfully.

"A regular freezer," promptly responded Tom,
clutching at the suggestion, and rubbing his hands
vigorously at the stove in emphasis thereof.

"Any news?"

"Not much.   Pretty dry."

"How's business?"

"Good.   *I* have got nothing to complain of."

"I'm glad of that.   And you're fortunate; for
the times are mighty hard."   The old gentleman
poked at the stove after saying this; and the result
of the move being summed up in the expression,
"I guess your fire needs more coal, Anna," he left
the room to get it. .

Mrs. Bayard and Lucy now came in; and the
latter and Anna took up their sewing, while the
old lady settled herself comfortably in a chair by
the stove.   She was a nice-looking old lady of
portly build; but there was no resemblance of the
daughters to either her or the father, which is not
an unusual occurrence.   Tom Griggs often studied
her face, with a view to find some feature thereof
to correspond with the beautiful countenance of
his darling; but he never succeeded.   He would

try to picture her as a girl, but always failed. The full and somewhat florid face, the gray hair, and the wrinkles were insurmountable barriers. He could not separate them from her, even with an imagination editorially trained ; and so he could not clothe her with youth. Odd queries often came into his mind when contemplating her. Was it possible she was ever young ? What was there about her that attracted her husband ? Did she love him as Anna loved ? Did he love her as Anna was loved ? Did she use to lie in his arms ? Did she use to watch anxiously for him ? Did he call her " darling " ? Were they ever different from what they were now ? Were they ever any thing but prosy and commonplace ? They could not have been. If so, they would not be prosy and commonplace now. These queries and speculations never led to any thing but the most hopeless chaos in Tom's mind ; and he found it was as difficult to clothe the couple with sentiment as with youth, and he would give up the struggle in despair, only to return to it again at the first opportunity. If they were not prosy and commonplace in their courting-days, how could they be so now ? He was quite confident it must have been a very dreary courtship.

Perhaps it was.

She called him Bayard, and he called her " old lady." There was certainly not much romance about *that.*

Again thrown in his mental wrestle with the

old enemy, Tom thanked his stars for the brighter future before him, and turned his eyes upon the dear girl. As his glance fell from the shapely head to the lithe fingers plying the needle, he felt that his cup of happiness was full to the brim. Was there ever a woman so beautiful as she? Was it a real, actual fact, that *she* was his pledged bride, and would in a few days be his own dear wife? Tom's heart swelled to such a degree under the inspiration of this thought as to make his vest feel a trifle uncomfortable. And every little while the beautiful face would be lifted, and the grand eyes beam full of love upon him. Happy Tom Griggs!

And yet there was a shadow upon his joy. Tom loved the nimble fingers so dearly, that he could not bear to have them tasked with sewing. If he were only rich! At any rate he would work hard himself, so hard that she should never have any thing to do. The dear face should never look tired after they were married, and the delicate hands never be marred by labor. When they were in their own home, he would take care of all that. There was a pleasure in thinking of it. It mattered not for himself. He could work himself to death, if necessary, to save her, the precious darling!

Foolish fellow! There were tears in his eyes as this thought came to him.

It was then Anna looked up again. She saw the tears, and a startled look flashed into her face.

But she saw also the light of a yearning devotion back of the glistening drops, and she knew it was his intense love for her that brought them; and she dropped her eyes again, while the look of joy in her face intensified. Mr. Bayard returned with the coal, with which he mended the fire, after convincing his wife that he was not desperately bent on mussing the carpet. Then he went back to the dining-room to smoke his pipe, and presently Mrs. Bayard followed him, to look after household duties. Lucy stitched on in silence. Tom noticed that she was very quiet, even for her; but, as it did not concern him, he made no comment.

"Tom, who was that young fellow that stood near the church-door as we were coming out last night?" asked Anna.

"What young fellow?"

"Why, didn't you see him? I don't see how you could help it. He was a stranger, and wore his hair rather long, and had on a cloak, and looked really romantic."

"Oh, him! That was Redner."

"Redner!" exclaimed Anna, looking up to her lover, "who's Redner?"

"He's the chap from Boston I hired Monday night," explained Tom. "Don't you know I told you of him when I came, — how he had detained me, and how I took him to be a poet?"

"Oh!" said Anna. And the subject dropped.

Soon after this, Lucy retired. When she was gone, Anna looked up, and lovingly whispered, —

"Come over here, Tom."

An entirely needless request; for, with that promptness peculiar to a wide-awake journalist, he was already on his way there.

It was surprising how close he could get to her without pushing her completely over.

"When will you be through, darling?" he asked, casting an unfriendly glance at the pile of sewing.

"In a little while. You know it must be done, Tom," she said, blushing as she looked up to him.

"I suppose it must," he reluctantly concurred; "but I want you to myself."

She stitched on a moment in silence. "Tom," she softly spoke, "why were there tears in your eyes a little while ago?"

He did not answer, and she raised her eyes to his face, — the eyes so full of intense love for him.

"Why was it, darling?"

"I cannot help it, pet; but, when I saw you at work, I wished that you might never have to do a single thing, and it made me feel badly to know that you were obliged to do this."

"But, Tom, work cannot hurt me." The idea that he thought it might filled her with joy. What a tender, thoughtful lover he was!

"But it hurts me to know you have to do it," he said. "When we are married, you will not have to slave at sewing; and I will work hard to get money, that you may not have to lift your hand to do a stroke."

"But, Tom, why should you work, and I not do any thing? Do you suppose I could rest with my hands folded while you were toiling day after day?"

"It matters not how hard I have to work, if you are saved."

"Don't it, Tom?" she whispered softly, pushing the hair slowly back from his forehead gently and lovingly; while he looked into the beautiful, earnest face, and felt how easy it would be to die, if necessary, for her dear sake.

"It is only two weeks now, Tom." He knew she referred to the wedding-day.

"Yes, only two weeks. I wish it was to-morrow."

"Do you, Tom?" she lovingly murmured, and then laid the beautiful head on his shoulder. "We will be so happy then in our own home. It will be such a pretty home: won't it, Tom?"

"Yes, darling."

"There are so many unhappy homes, Tom. I don't see how married people can live so. I believe it must be the woman's fault. If the wife tried to make the home pleasant, and kept herself neatly dressed, and had every thing in order, and didn't let the work drag, I *know* there would be a difference. Don't you think there would, Tom?"

Tom knew very well that love was the great incentive to domestic effort, and that these women

were not Annas, and that they could not, in consequence, very well do otherwise than they did;
but he did not say so. It was a matter entirely
outside of his future, and so it did not interest
him. It was pleasant to have her lie in his arms,
and to hear her talk; and so he kissed her lovingly,
and simply said, "Yes, dear one."

"O Tom! it is so delightful to think of our
home!" she exclaimed. "It will be small, of
course; but then it shall be a perfect gem of comfort and happiness. We will have pretty furniture, in bright colors, — real bright, — and some
pictures, and the cunningest kitchen. And, when
you are at the office, I will be to work in our home,
making it bright and cheerful for you when you
come home. I will have the table ready set, and
myself dressed; and then I will go out to the gate,
and stand there, and watch for you until you come.
O Tom! won't it be so grand?" She lifted her
head from its support, and clapped the pretty
hands in an ecstasy of delight, while her eyes
shone with the pleasurable emotions the picture
created.

"My darling!" was all he said; but the intensity
of the utterance spoke volumes. He drew her
tighter to his breast, too full of joy himself to
speak a word.

"And, Tom," she went on, "I'll be so proud to
bring you into the dining-room, and show you the
table. I know just how I will have it arranged."

"Do you, pet?"

"Yes, Tom. I think there is a great deal in the way a table is set. Some tables look as if the things were just thrown on to them; and some don't look as if there was any thing on at all, and look so bare and bleak that I wonder how a man can have the patience to stand it. I want our table to have a snowy white cloth, and cut glass, and nice stone china for breakfast and dinner, and real china for tea; and napkins with holders; and silver spoons and forks; and I will crochet pretty mats for the vegetable dishes and tea and coffee pot; and we will want a silver sugar-spoon and a silver butter-knife; and then— O Tom!" she cried, springing erect again in the excitement of the anticipation, "won't it be perfectly *grand?*"

He caught her to his breast, and bent silently over the flushed, happy face. Something touched her cheek.

"O Tom! are you crying?" was her startled whisper.

"It is all so bright, so beautiful, dear one!" he said in a broken voice.

She made no reply; but she put both of her arms tightly about his neck, and her cheeks grew wet with her own tears.

Happy, happy lovers!—oblivious to all the rest of the world,—unconscious even of time.

It was the striking of the clock that aroused them.

"Why, Tom! that is one o'clock!"

By a gigantic effort he wrenched himself from the

dream, and came down upon reality on both feet with a force that jarred his entire system, got his hat, gave her a final embrace and a shower of kisses, and then went out into the chilling night-air to wrestle with the frost and an aggressive conscience.

CHAPTER VII.

DOCKERTY.

IT was the Sunday-morning service at the church Mrs. Quimby attended. We say *Mrs.* Quimby, because her lord rarely graced the structure with his presence. He was a member; but it was so long since his conversion, that its significance was about obliterated. Then it always happened, singularly enough, that there was something to do about the house, something to look after out of the house, or something out of the way with his health or the weather, when the church was holding service. To a close observer it looked very much as if the church was in this manner robbing Mr. Quimby of valuable opportunities to develop his spiritual strength.

At any rate, it was evident that he had been robbed.

A peculiarity of Mr. Quimby's case was the fact, that, while these circumstances appeared to be all-powerful, yet there was a season in nearly every year during which they were utterly powerless to prevail over him. This season was the revival period. During the progress of a revival, the church graciously permitted Mr. Quimby to rise superior to every ordinary circumstance, as well as a number that were extraordinary. He grew with the revival. As it progressed, he advanced in zeal. He also declined with it.

Mr. Quimby was in the closest sympathy with a revival. Scarcely a prayer-meeting would he miss, although one was held every evening in the week. When a man gets up at an unusual early hour of a summer morning, he is apt to lose patience with those people who will persist in lying abed. So Mr. Quimby, in his faithful attendance upon the revival services, lost patience with those church-members who were not equally faithful, even in so great a degree as to become sore vexed with them.

So, too, Mrs. Quimby, whom a state of chronic illness prevented from venturing out in the night-air when there was no excitement in Zion, was faithful in her attendance upon the every-night meetings that were now in progress. And the excellent lady, being surcharged with the grace which had silently accumulated in the other portions of the year, supplemented her faith by her works in earnestly exhorting all about her to "get religion."

Both Mr. and Mrs. Quimby were absent this Sunday morning; and their pew was equally divided between Dockerty and a strange lady whom the sexton had seated therein, or, as Dockerty expressed it on getting home, "had run in," — an act he indignantly resented.

Dockerty, by the way, was the only son of Mr. and Mrs. Quimby, also their only child. Chronologically he was aged eight years : in the development of mental perception and in the matter of human experience, he was somewhat older. Dockerty had appeared in this world several years after the immediate friends of his parents had given up his coming at all, and there had been no second edition.

At the time of his birth, on the very day in fact, an aged maiden lady came into possession, by purchase, of the property whereon Mrs. Quimby sustained the lives of her family and some dozen boarders. The new purchaser lived in the neighborhood, owned several buildings, which she rented ; and having no apparent avocation, or trouble in paying her bills, was naturally enough reputed to be enormously wealthy. The name of this elderly lady was Dockerty, — Miss Anabel Dockerty.

It was rather remarkable that she should become possessed of the house on the very day that the Quimbys became possessed of their heir. Mrs. Quimby, who was of a religious turn, could not fail of seeing the hand of Providence in this, pointing unmistakably to the naming of the child. It was an indication that to her amounted to the importance of a command, and she hastened to obey. The boy was called Dockerty Quimby, and very frequently called by the first half of the name in clear, resonant. tones, from the frontstoop of the house, whenever he was needed from the street.

It might be mentioned, incidentally, that Miss Dockerty lived just across the way.

To his mother Dockerty was the chief hope of life. To his father he presented a most intricate problem. To both he was a good-sized handful.

On this sabbath morning, Dockerty, with his hair clipped so short as to show quite an expanse of scalp, and his face shining with an almost unearthly lustre, sat on the seat of the pew, with one leg under him, and in a position to bring his profile in view of the choir, and to enable his eyes to take in, in turn, the profile of the lady who had the honor of sharing the pew with him. For some five minutes Dockerty occupied himself in contemplating her, looking carefully first over her apparel, and then concentrating his gaze upon her . face. Without even so much as the quiver of an eyelid, he engaged in this survey, and then suddenly, as if violently struck with the recurrence of an idea, he unfolded his under leg, dove his hand into his breeches-pocket, and immediately brought forth an object that completely engrossed his attention. For a moment he remained in rapt contemplation of it; and then he held it up between his thumb and forefinger, so as to get the very best light possible upon it. It also happened, undesignedly without doubt, that in this position it became plain to the view of all the congregation sitting back of him.

It was a five-cent coin (a new one at that), and it glistened in the light. For a moment or more

Dockerty thus held it up, turning it from side to side, and viewing it most intently.

Gradually a shadow fell upon his face. Slowly it deepened, until his entire countenance was lost in its depth. The hand with the coin was brought back to his knee. There was a great trouble on Dockerty's mind. That it was not caused by the nickel, but came rather from reflections in connection therewith, was evident from the sorrowful fondness of the gaze he fixed upon it.

It was in a spirit of great irritation that he mumbled to himself, —

"I hates the heathen, I do. Heathen's hogs. Whattuv I got to do with 'em? Whatsit to me about heathen? What righttuv they got to be comin' aroun' an' scoopin' up *my* five cents?"

Dockerty stared about him with a dreadfully morose expression. His little face was as dark as night. He fairly quivered under a powerful sense of his wrongs, and his voice showed in its intensity the depth of the outraged feelings it gave utterance to.

"A new five cents too!" It is utterly impossible to convey to the reader a tithe of the anguish imparted in this reflection. "A bran new five cents, or I'm a sucker!" he explosively added. "An' this to go to the heathen! How them little naked coots will grin an' kick up when they see it!" Dockerty groaned, and his body writhed as if in mortal agony. "They'll go off an' buy things with it, an' stuff 'emselves till they're ready to bust. An' what's the good? I'm a good mind ter spend it myself; that's what I'm a good mind ter do. I'm just as good as a heathen, if I do wear clothes. But nobody gets pennies for *me*, an' talks about *me*, an' makes pictures in books of *me*. I won't stand this much longer, I can tell you. I ain't agoin' to have my money scooped up like this. Ain't I as good as a heathen, — a little nasty black thing, what takes all the boys' pennies for candy, an' never has no worms? Ugh!" Dockerty, on making this ejaculation, scowled in such a frightful manner, that the strange lady, happening to observe him, was so worked upon, that she precipitately retired from the pew, and took one far removed.

The young man watched this movement with an expression of gloomy abstraction upon his face, but made no comment.

"Ugh!" he presently repeated. "Hot old heathens them be, with their naked bodies, an' rings in their noses! Why don't they go to work, an' earn their own pennies? What do they keep a comin' aroun' after mine for? Darn 'em! They gets my pennies, an' then buys things for to stuff 'emselves with, an' goes aroun' jumpin' over hydrants, an' stonin' dogs an' hens, an' catchin' on behind sleighs; an' I've got to be starched as stiff as a poker, an' sit up here as straight as a stick, a-lookin' at the minister. I'm a good mind ter be a heathen myself, there's so much money in it."

He looked anxiously through the window upon the wintry air, and sighed regretfully.

"If it wa'n't so cold, I'd just rip off my pants this very minit, an scoot aroun' town like a house afire." The sudden animation that lighted up his face as suddenly died out, and he sighed again. "What's the good if I did? No one wouldn't give me a cent. I ain't black, I ain't dirty, I ain't far off; I'm too close to town to be a heathen."

A rustle at the opening of the pew directed his attention in that direction; and he saw Lucy Bayard enter, and seat herself. Dockerty's face softened as her own sweet face brightened into sudden sunshine in recognition of his glance. He crept up to her side at once.

"Miss Bayard, do you see that?" He held the glittering coin up to her view.

"Yes, Dockerty," she whispered.

"That," he moaned, "is agoin' to the heathen."

"To the heathen?"

"To the heathen," he despairingly uttered, "or I'm a busted pickle-jar."

With this deplorable picture of his condition in the event of the miscarriage of the coin, he subsided into a long train of gloomy thought; one hand clinching the treasure, and the other mechanically engaged in rubbing the top of his head.

While Dockerty wrestled with his responsibility to the heathen, a pair of very restless eyes, four seats back, were roaming over the congregation. The owner of the eyes was Mr. George Redner, the new journeyman in "The Gazette" office. Being a stranger, and somewhat out of the com-

mon appearance of the Gallowhill young men, he
became an object of much attention to the very
young ladies in the choir at his back, and the
other very young ladies who rarely sit with their
parents, but appear to congregate by instinct in
the rear pews. To all these the young man had
a peculiar attraction ; and, when his eyes swept
their vicinity, it was to be confronted by many
fully opened maiden orbs.

It was thus he was occupied when a figure
passed down the aisle, and so close to him that he
could have touched it where he sat. One glance
showed him that it was Lucy Bayard.

During the balance of the service, his whole
attention was concentrated on the Quimbys' pew.
Not a rustle of a ribbon, not a motion of her person, escaped the eyes which had now lost their rest-
lessness, and were completely absorbed in the quiet
figure of the young girl. He envied Dockerty his
proximity to her, all unconscious of the brooding
misery that darkened that young man's heart, and
which made him entirely oblivious to the sweet
delight of his position so close to Lucy Bayard.
To Redner there was an approach to a halo about
the bristling hairs and the expanse of scalp. Dear
Dockerty ! What a nice boy he was ! What a
well-shaped head ! What intelligent ears ! Other
portions of his person were equally delightful to
the contemplation without doubt ; but the back of
the pew shut out, unfortunately, all but his head
and ears from Redner's enraptured view.

Lucy scarcely moved during the delivery of the sermon. Redner hoped that she would look around that he might feast on a full view of her face, or turn to Dockerty that he might lunch generously, as it were, on her profile; but she did neither. She was all absorbed in the discourse, and never once removed her eyes from the speaker.

When the service closed, the young man lingered long enough to have her step into the aisle, and thus face him. Then their eyes met, and hers dropped at once. He gave one all-intense glance into the sweet face, and then hurried into the porch, and out on the walk. Here he took place with a crowd of young men, who were as much at ease in front of the door as if they had been born into that position, and who were contemplating the outcoming people with devout attention, and watched for her to appear.

In a moment or two she came down the stair to the walk, and moved away to her home. He concentrated his gaze upon her with all-devouring intensity; but she did not look toward him again. She passed on, and he followed after, keeping her in range of his admiring vision until she reached her door. And after that he passed the house three or four times at a slow pace, with his gaze lingering on the structure; but he was not gratified with another glimpse of her person.

CHAPTER VIII.

AT TEA AT QUIMBY'S.

REDNER was washing up for tea one evening, when Mr. Phillips said to him, —

"You want to slick up your very best to-night; for there's going to be company to supper.".

"Who's that?" asked Redner, towelling his face.

"Lucy Bayard," said Phillips.

It was perhaps the friction of the towel that made the young man's face look so red.

"How do you know?" came from the folds of that article.

"I see her downstairs when I came in."

"But she may not be going to stay here to tea."

"I guess there ain't any doubt of it," said Phillips; "for she's got her things off."

This settled it, of course, and nothing more was said. But Redner was full fifteen minutes in arranging his hair, and adjusting his necktie. He followed Phillips downstairs in a state of great anxiety.

The Quimbys and their boarders were at the table, and with her back to him, as he entered the door, sat Lucy. He did not need to see her face to tell him that it was she. The shapely head, the graceful shoulders, the mass of richly colored hair lying in massive braid adown her back, revealed to him in a flash her presence.

Mrs. Quimby had left a seat between Lucy and herself, and nodded to Redner to take it. We are not quite sure that Mrs. Quimby was a schemer, — at least, any more so than a married woman of her years is expected to be. It was apparent to her, as well as to another, that both were young, and that both were unmarried. From this knowledge she had instinctively worked herself into the belief that both must some time look matrimony square in the face. So she seated them as she did, and had them both under her matronly survey, and was quite pleased thereat.

Mrs. Quimby presented him to her. The beautiful smile flashed up, and illuminated the grave face, as she acknowledged the ceremony, and went out as quickly as it came, leaving her cheeks flushed as if from the light of its glory, and her eyes bent down upon her plate.

As was hinted in the preceding chapter, there was considerable of an awakening in the church where the Quimbys worshipped. Under the impulse of the movement, Mr. and Mrs. Quimby were shining conspicuously, having thrown aside their candle, and rented an entire calcium-light. This was particularly so with the excellent landlady, about whose presence the odor of sanctity was excelled only by that of arnica. Her zeal was admirable. There was, she contended, a time for all things. The time for levity, for idleness, for vanity, had gone by. It was now time to look after the solemn interests of the soul. Mrs. Quimby's mind was firmly held in the clamps of this conviction. She wanted everybody to get religion. She urged them with indescribable pathos to lay hold of it. She overflowed with zeal.

Mrs. Quimby was on the popular current, with sails full set; and she floated majestically onward, one of the proudest vessels afloat, — although not a vessel of wrath, as she looked at the matter. To her religion was a choice tidbit, — something like a new piece of furniture, or a late style in hat, or a very pretty design in dress-goods, — the enjoyment of whose possession consisted mainly in having other people know she had it. The subject was largely treated of at this tea, as it was, for the matter of that, at all teas during the white heat of the interest. With the day ended and the family gathered about the table, the freedom from toil and the thought thereof made it a specially favorable opportunity for the presentment of a serious subject. To Mrs. Quimby it was a particularly felicitous occasion for airing her piety. And on this, as on all other occasions, she was ably assisted by a tall, spare young lady, who delved in millinery, and who was chiefly noted for a pair of hard gray eyes, and the frequent repetition of the ejaculation, "Ahem!" which she gave with touching pathos.

Mrs. Quimby found in Mr. Phillips an available agent also, — not that that gentleman was in sympathetic accord with her views : very much to the contrary, we fear. But Mrs. Quimby used him on special occasions to lift her up to the proper conversational plane, in which office Mr. Phillips operated somewhat in the character of a derrick.

On this occasion that worthy gentleman was seated at the side of a young lady who aided in the manufacture of paper-boxes through the day, and who was now completing her second week in the Quimby mansion. She was a young person of quiet demeanor, and with a face not particularly noticeable in any feature but the eyes, which were large and slightly staring, and in color might have been vulgarly described as "buttermilk."

On her first appearance in the house, the susceptible Ezekiah was struck most favorably, and lost no time in improving on the introduction. That he was in turn flatteringly considered by the young lady, there could be no doubt, although he was not aware of the same, and was in consequence considerably torn by doubt, and elevated by hope, and crushed by despair. In other words, Mr. Phillips' soul was passing through a violent siege of love in its fever-and-ague stages. He felt, as he took his seat at the table and gave the slim young lady a rapturous glance, that he must know his fate before morning. He was in a situation that made it imperatively necessary that he should have this knowledge. To be frank, Mr.

Phillips had a full-sheet poster in three colors to get out the next day; and he was certain he could not do it full justice with his mind in this chaotic quiver. He was contemplating this contingency when Mrs. Quimby's voice aroused him.

"You was at church last night, wasn't you, Mr. Phillips?"

"Yes'm," he said, starting from his revery.

"Didn't you think it was a splendid meeting?" she next inquired.

"Pretty lively," he replied, passing the young lady the dried beef and a look of unutterable affection.

Mrs. Quimby paused a moment, and quizzingly eyed the sugar-bowl, as if in some doubt of the appropriateness of the term "lively" in this connection. But she rallied.

"Didn't it almost make you wish that you had religion, Mr. Phillips?" she insinuatingly questioned.

"I don't know — I hadn't — I — I couldn't say," stammered Mr. Phillips, flushing to the very roots of his hair, and trying his utmost to twist his face into a propitiatory smile, while he was delivering this plausible explanation.

It was a remarkable reply from him. In his normal condition of feeling he would have decisively, if not irreverently, answered in the negative; but his present state of mind was softened to a degree that was nearly akin to religion, and he was not quite certain but that he desired it.

He was not the first man, perhaps, to mistake a love-sentiment for a religious emotion.

"I'll bet you had serious thoughts on it," said Mrs. Quimby, with a glance that might have looked like cunning were it not for the great delicacy of her expression. "Nobody could set under such preaching as that of last night, an' have the Word presented as it was by him, an' hear them prayers, an' not feel as if they was sinners, an' needed grace right away. It was just glorious! I don't think I was ever at a meeting where there was so much feeling as there was there last night. God was there, or I don't know what's what. It seemed to me as if the very roof was a comin' off. Didn't it seem so to you, Miss Hervisson?"

The party addressed was the possessor of the hard gray eyes, and she hastened to respond, —

"Why, my—ahem! I was perfectly carried away with it. I thought Brother Edgett was perfectly grand— per-fect-ly grand, —ahem! He spoke so feelingly, so impressively; and he has *such* a voice, —ahem! You could see that every word came right from his very soul. Didn't you think so, Mrs. Quimby? ahem!"

"I should say I did!" exclaimed Mrs. Quimby with enthusiasm. "If there ever was a man in dead earnest, he is. Why" (looking all around the table), "you could see he meant every word he said by his very looks. Every time he swung his arms, he showed what he was. Oh, he was splendid! I wish you could a' heard him, Lucy, because he's just the kind of preacher to suit you. You will go with us to-night to hear him: won't you, dear?"

"Not to-night, thank you, Mrs. Quimby," she answered. She saw her hostess's design, and shrank from it.

Mrs. Quimby was disappointed, but she made no comment.

"You'll go, Mr. Redner: won't you?" she asked.

He wanted to refuse, as Lucy was not going, but consented before he could recover himself.

"I hope, Mr. Phillips, that you and Miss Hurley will come too."

Mr. Phillips hastened to assure her, that, if agreeable to the young lady, he would cheerfully comply. The young lady graciously admitted that it would be agreeable.

Upon this, Mrs. Quimby's face fairly shone with delight at the success of this arrangement, which promised so much of enjoyment to those concerned; and there was a grain of exultation in her manner as she said, —

"I think we should do all we can to help along the cause. We must sow our seed, as the pastor says, even if we don't see any fruit. We can't always tell what will come of it; but we must keep on doing all the same, an' God will take care of it. I got religion when I was a girl, an' I've wished often that I had got it afore. Religion is the best thing anybody can get hold of. It

helps 'em, an' makes 'em feel good. I don't know
what I'd a' done with all my trials an' troubles
an' sickness, if it warn't for religion to comfort
an' stay me. It has been the only thing that's
kept me up, an' it has made me so happy hundreds
of times! I feel so good now, I can't tell any
thing about it. But I want more religion: we all
want more of it. It's something nobody had
oughter be without."

"Glory to God!" ejaculated her husband in a
mahogany sort of voice.

"So I say, Reuben: glory to God!" she spirit-
edly returned. "An' may He come down an' take
hold of the hardened hearts, an' shake 'em up,
until every one in the world has got religion. Oh!
why don't people get it? Why will they keep
puttin' it off, an' puttin' it off, until it is too late?
'Now is the accepted time; now is the day of sal-
vation.'" Mrs. Quimby sighed, and contemplated
the cream-jug.

"Ahem!" observed Miss Hervisson in a tone
of sympathy.

"What a happy day that will be," murmured
the landlady, as if communing with herself, "when
every man an' woman an' child willuv got religion,
when they all put away the things of the flesh," —
here her eyes mechanically strayed to the dried
beef which was being put away, — "and give their
whole hearts to" —

"Ma, I love God," Dockerty took occasion to
mention at this juncture; and, as he said it, he

looked around the table for marks of the approval he was confident he had won.

"Then," continued his. mother without noting the interruption, "we'll see a much different world than this.   Now, don't you really think so yourself, Mr. Phillips?"

That gentleman was on the point of making a suitable response, when Dockerty at once put in, with some asperity, —

"Say, ma, I love God, I tell you!"

"Dockerty," said his mother sternly, "I have asked Mr. Phillips a question, an' I want you to keep quiet."

"Well, when I say I do, I do!" repeated the perverse youth.

"Dockerty, if you don't keep still, I will give you a setting up that you'll remember."

"Then, why don't you hear me when I tell you I do?" he crossly demanded.

"I did hear you."

"Give me some cake, then," was the sullen rejoinder.

The cake was passed by the frowning woman; and Mr. Phillips undertook to say — the diversion having drawn the eager attention of all to him — that he had no doubt of it.

After this very satisfactory exposition of his views on the question, the family rose from the table, and the various atoms thereof dispersed, to make ready for the evening service.

CHAPTER IX.

MR. PHILLIPS MEETS AN EMERGENCY.

In the privilege of escorting Miss Hurley to church, the foreman of "The Gazette" was exalted to a degree of buoyancy rarely attained even by a balloon. He was confident she was a most estimable young woman, and he felt that matters had progressed to a stage which demanded that he should win her. In the light of her countenance the dark record of past defeats and heartaches melted from both sight and memory, and his whole nature went out to her with all the gush of a first and only love.

He knew that he never had loved, and never again could love, like this; and to win her was not only desirable, but absolutely necessary. It was necessary for the peace of his mind in the present, and for his welfare in the vastness of eternity. This was very strong ground, but Mr. Phillips knew it was proper ground.

He was in a flutter of delight all the way to the church, and through the service, of which he heard but precious little, and understood very much less, we are sorry to state.

It is gratifying to record that Miss Hurley acted throughout it all in a most creditable manner, showing no uneasiness, no alarm, no distress. It might be said of her that she bore herself with a heroism that was admirable.

She kept her eyes steadily fixed upon the clergyman, and evidently took in every sentence with keen relish ; while poor Mr. Phillips sat in a quiver of whirling thought, hardly realizing where he was, or comprehending what it was all about that was going on around him.

At the close of the service his nervousness became more apparent. It seemed as if he could not get her out on the street where he could have her all alone to himself soon enough. It is singular that Miss Hurley was so calm and serene. She moved from the building as if she had a fortnight at her disposal for that purpose. Once on the street, Mr. Phillips' nervous exuberance was somewhat toned down by the proximity of the ordeal he had voluntarily taken upon himself to endure. It is not at all likely that Miss Hurley anticipated, in the least degree, the purpose of her companion. On the contrary, there was much in her demeanor to indicate that she did not. She spoke feelingly of the sermon, and said she had been so interested in it, she was sure she had not lost a single sentence. Then she wanted to know who that was who sat two seats ahead of them in the left aisle, and anxiously inquired what he thought of the singing of the second hymn.

At the first inquiry Mr. Phillips had great difficulty in suppressing a groan. He could not understand how it was possible for her to hear that sermon with himself at her side. As to such a hideously irrelevant matter as the identity of the party two seats ahead in the left aisle, he had not given the faintest thought. In fact, he had not seen him at all, and hoped, with a sincerity that could not be questioned, that he never would see him — alive. Of the hymn he had not heard a single line. It might have been a Brazilian polka on an instrument with one string, so far as his knowledge ran. Something a thousand times more important than all this filled his mind, and held captive his every thought.

It would be a dreadful thing indeed, if, after all his dreaming of winning her, she should be wanting in the necessary reciprocal sentiment. But Mr. Phillips could not now abandon making a protestation of the intense affection he held in his heart for her, and learning her feeling toward him. Under this conviction he took occasion to slap himself on the breast in a subdued manner, and to charge himself with great feeling to —

"Brace up!"

"Did you speak, Mr. Phillips?" inquired Miss Hurley gently.

"No — that is — oh, no, I did not speak!" he hastened to explain, visibly disturbed by the thought that she should have heard him.

There was a moment of silence. Every step

was taking them nearer home. Mr. Phillips felt
that now or never he must take the momentous
step. He was not in an enviable frame of mind.
The knowledge of his physical failing in an emergency of this nature came upon him with unpleas-
ant force. There was a faint hope in his breast
that time, the great healer, had either effected a
complete cure of the trouble, or greatly modified it.
The uncertainty was dreadful.

Mr. Phillips walked on with the young lady,
every step increasing his mental misery. She
asked him several questions concerning his im-
pressions of the meeting; but his answers were so
vague and disjointed, and contained so little bearing on the subject, that even the very moderate
young lady could not fail to be awakened thereby.
Mr. Phillips knew he was not giving intelligible
answers; but he could not help himself. As he
subsequently remarked to a sympathetic friend, of
his tongue, "It just wobbled in my mouth." With
his whole mind concentrated on one subject, his
tongue could not intelligently dwell upon any
other; and he saw that further endeavors to respond were only increasing the disturbance. If
he was to come to the point at all, he must do it
at once. With this pressure upon him, he plunged
into the abyss.

"Matilda," he began. The very sound of his
voice so startled him, that for an instant he paused.
It was so strange, so hard, and so unnatural, that it
sounded as if coming from beneath an unoccupied

building, while its ascent of his throat seemed to
raise a cloud of dust the entire way.

"Matilda," he repeated with another effort, "do
you know how long it is since we first see each
other?"

Miss Hurley contracted her brow as if in a
pang of desperate thought.

"Why, I really don't remember," she answered.

"It will be three weeks to-night," said Mr. Phillips huskily.

"Can it be possible? I had forgotten all about
it." This was false, we are sorry to say. Miss
Hurley knew it was three weeks to almost an
hour.

"Yes, three weeks ago to-night," repeated Mr.
Phillips. "Do you know what I just said to myself the first time I saw you?" The speaker
glanced tenderly on his companion.

"When you first saw me, Mr. Phillips?"

"Yes, Matilda." It was wonderful the depth
of tenderness in the utterance of the name,
although much of it was obscured by the huski-
ness of his voice.

"I don't know, I am sure, Mr. Phillips."

"Well, I says to myself, says I — says I, 'There's
a true lady for you; there's style.' That's what I
said." Mr. Phillips threw out his chest under the
inspiration of this reflection, and looked very
steadily up the street.

"Why, I don't see how you could tell any thing
about me on so short an acquaintance; for you had

just seen me, you know." Miss Hurley was
nevertheless pleased by such appreciation of her
worth, despite the surprise she felt at its expression.

"I can't help it," protested the foreman of "The
Gazette," with fervor. "That's what I thought, an'
that's what I said; an' I stand by it now, and a
hundred times more, by Judas!" Mr. Phillips'
long and solemn features shone like a new hearse.

"O Mr. Phillips!" cried the maiden, very much
shocked, "don't swear: please don't."

"Why, that ain't swearing, Matilda," earnestly
protested Mr. Phillips. "Just saying Ju—"

"Oh, please don't!" she pleaded, clinging closely
to his arm.

"I won't, if you don't want me to," he hastened
to assure her. "I'll do any thing to please you.
May Heaven split me open with a cold chisel
if"—

"O Mr. Phillips! don't, *don't*, DON'T! It is so
dreadful to have you talk like that."

Mr. Phillips immediately subsided, partly from
doubting his ability to convey an adequate idea of
his fervor in language attuned to her delicate ear,
and partly from the delight he experienced in
having her clinging so helplessly to him.

"Matilda," he presently resumed, after a violent
effort with his throat, "I have got something —
that is, I mean there is something — something I
want to say." He stopped short at this juncture,
while the perspiration started out on his forehead

in very large drops.   Like a discreet girl, she kept still.

"I," he began again, and then coughed, "I want to ask you if— if— if—" Mr. Phillips went off on a series of *ifs*, while his eyes protruded to an unnatural degree, and his nose and cheek-bones and chin appeared in glaring prominence.   It was only by clutching his throat in a prompt and vigorous manner that he was able to stem the dreadful flood of conjunctions that· poured from his lips. The effort caused him to stand still, and gasp for breath.

It was a rather embarrassing position for a young lady.   Miss Hurley felt that something of a striking nature was imminent; but whether her hopes or her fears were to be fulfilled, she could not determine.   If she had the hope of a great brightness coming into her life, to cast its sunshine upon her path forevermore, there was also the fear that some terrible physical casualty would come to blight it.   Really, Mr. Phillips did show strong symptoms of having a fit right there in the street.   Unfortunate as was his condition, hers was infinitely worse.

"Matilda," he gasped, after walking a few steps farther, "I want to ask you if you do —that is, if you could—"

Mr. Phillips could give no utterance beyond this.   His jaws twitched, his tongue rattled, his eyes protruded; but no expression came from it all, — that is, in words — although his features, even in the dim snowlight, showed eloquently enough the force of his convictions. The dreadful weakness had struck Mr. Phillips, and he · could not overcome it. He felt the pit of his stomach giving away; but he could not avert the disaster. A cold, clammy perspiration bedewed his face, while his limbs trembled to a degree that threatened their usefulness.

One more gigantic effort he made to throw off the demon that was riding his soul to its death.

" Matilda," he tremulously began, " it is three weeks since first we met. Since then you and me have been often together, Matilda. We've lived right in the same house together, and seen one another four or five times a day every day. You ain't no stranger to me, Matilda: are you, Matilda?" His voice began to falter at this juncture.

" No, Mr. Phillips," she softly replied, clinging closer to his arm, but looking down to the walk.

His voice was very thick and unsteady when he began again : —

" Then, Matilda, do you think you do — I mean do you think that you could — could — could —" He broke completely down.

" Could what, Mr. Phillips?" she whispered.

" Could — could —" he stuttered, shaking violently, " could you lo— lo—" They had reached the gate. " Could — could — c-o-u-l-d!"

The last utterance was a prolonged howl of impotency; and with it the thoroughly disgusted and completely unhinged lover dropped her arm, and fled up the street at his highest possible speed.

For a moment Miss Hurley stood at the gate, and looked after the retreating form in petrified amazement; and then, partly recovering her senses, and suddenly realizing that she had miraculously escaped a horrible fate at the hands of an impending lunatic, she precipitately retired within doors, and lost no time in gaining the protection of her own room.

The flying Mr. Phillips abated not his speed until he reached the main street. Once there, he made directly to the hotel, and entered the bar in a stage of exhaustion that rendered him powerless to speak. He went up to the counter, and leaned heavily over it, catching desperately for breath, while his long and prominent features bore an appearance of such ghastly dismay that the bar-tender immediately parted with his wits. He could only stare at him, too amazed to speak.

"Ci— cider brandy!" gasped Mr. Phillips.

The decanter and glass were promptly placed before him.

"Pour it."

The bar-tender hastened to obey.

Ezekiah grasped the vessel, and shot its contents down his throat.

"Another," was all he said.

He was again helped.

"What's the matter, Ez?" asked the bar-tender, seeing that he was reviving, and taking on a more natural look. "Haven't been hoisting in any poison, have yer?"

"Joseph," said Mr. Phillips, with great impressiveness, and leaning so far over the bar as to threaten to cleave Joseph's face with his sharp nose, "there's some things which should never be permitted to escape the sanctity of the human breast. *This is one of 'em.*" Mr. Phillips hereupon straightened himself, made a dignified flourish with his right hand, and gravely repeated, "This is one of 'em."

With that he solemnly retired. But his composure was but momentary, and came only from the necessity of sustaining himself in the presence of others. Alone on the street, his courage left him; and, smiting his dishonest and recreant stomach, he bitterly cried, —

"If Heaven would only send me a camel, I'd scoot away, and be at peace!"

CHAPTER X.

THE WEDDING-EVE.

THERE never was a more devoted lover than Tom Griggs. And so thoughtful and tender was he in his wooing, that the most indifferent in such matters could not fail to notice; and even Redner, with his professed advanced ideas of gallantry, was deeply affected thereby. Rain or shine Tom never missed his evening; and they never went out into company or to an entertainment without going together. It was a genuine pleasure to see him in the rain give her four-fifths of the umbrella, and composedly take the drops on his own defenceless person. It was solid comfort to note the readiness with which he would carry her Bible when escorting her from church, for fear the burden of the volume would tire her; while it was the summit of delight to watch with what tenderness he would adjust her wraps, and bundle her up so that not a breath of the cruel winter air should touch the delicate form. Tom Griggs' greatest joy was found in doing for his darling.

But now the end of the dreary waiting was drawing nigh. Day succeeded day at that dignified pace with which time approaches an intensely desired goal, and the eve of the wedding-day had finally come. Tom Griggs knew that there never had been, and never could be, so happy a man as was he. He moved about and looked around in a sort of mild delirium. He watched her every step as she went about the little sitting-room getting this and that together for the morrow, and looked upon the flushed, happy face, and wondered to himself if it were possible that the long-hoped-for, earnestly-yearned-after night had really come, — the eve of their wedding-day.

A thousand times he had pictured it, and what he would do, and what she would do, and what he would feel, and what he would say, and how she would look. It had been a bright, beautiful picture to him, so beautiful really that there were times when he was led to doubt its ever coming. But it was here *now.* Very startling, to be sure, and almost improbable, but still it had come; and here he sat and greedily watched her every motion, and there she was, his beautiful darling, right before his eyes, and never looking more beautiful or less real.

It was a dazed condition of mind he was in, and it seemed that he must not stir, or the vision would dissolve into nothing; and yet he wanted to take hold of her, and assure himself in a most substantial manner that it was all an actual fact.

There was much for her to do in picking up the odds and ends left from the day's work; but by and by the last article was laid away in its place, the last thread was picked up from the carpet, and then she went to him, and sat down on his lap, and put her arms around his neck, and her mouth close to his ear, and whispered, —

"Darling, I have got something to show you. Do you want to see it?"

For a moment he made no reply, but held her silently, but with eloquent tenderness, in his arms.

"What do you want to show me, pet?"

"Do you *really* want to see it?" she asked, trying at the same time to look as if it were possible that he shouldn't want to.

"Certainly I do. What is it?"

"Come with me."

She took up the lamp, and led him into the parlor. She sat the light down, approached a chair, removed from it a garment, and displayed it before him, her eyes glistening with pride and expectation.

"O my darling, how beautiful it is!" he rapturously exclaimed.

Indeed it was beautiful. They were to be married the next morning at ten o'clock, and shortly after were to start on their trip. The wedding-silk was to be packed up for the journey, and she was to be married in her travelling-dress. And here it was. It was an ashes-of-roses color, trimmed with satin of a corresponding shade; and it was made up in the very latest style, and that, to Tom, appeared to be the climax of dressmaking art.

It was a wonderfully pretty dress; and as she held it against her shapely form, and beamed over its top upon him with her grand eyes, he just preserved sufficient calmness to realize that this glorious picture was all, all his, and then in a flash he had her and the delicate robe in one confused mass in his arms.

The surprised girl had no chance to give the faintest expression to the horror she felt at the sacrilege to the garment, nor to make the least move to save it. It was all she was able to do to keep her breath through the ordeal, and was even inclined to be thankful that she came forth as whole as she did.

"Did I hurt it, darling?" he asked with exasperating anxiety.

"O Tom!" cried she, looking aghast at the mussed robe, "how could you?"

It was a cruel thing to have done, and the culprit should have given evidence of the liveliest penitence. But he didn't. On the contrary, there was an undisguised twinkle of amusement in his eyes. Looking up, she caught it.

"What a great awkward bear you are!" she exclaimed; and then she laughed outright.

In a flash she was again struggling in the great, strong arms, and the sacred dress was lying in a crumpled heap on the carpet.

At the moment a tap came at the door; and Lucy's beautiful smile, lighting up the quiet face, immediately appeared. Tom let go of his treasure in an instant, and promptly sobered down into a degree of behavior that was quite comforting to the sorely tried Anna.

Lucy came in to see what he thought of the dress, and was even startled out of her quiet air by the condition it was in, but was too discreet to make any comments. The sisters smoothed its ruffled folds, and spoke of its excellences; and Lucy asked Tom if he didn't think the dressmaker had done marvellously, and Tom said she certainly had, although he mentally explained to himself, as a sort of compromise with his pride, that she could not very well have done less, with such a perfect model to work upon.

To Lucy the garment was scarcely less a delight than to the dawning bride. Wedding-garments and baby-clothes have a claim peculiar to themselves upon a woman's heart. This is not shared with any thing else, or affected by any thing else. It is an isolated attachment, and lasts while life exists. To Lucy the travelling-dress in which her sister was on the morrow to begin a new existence revived no memories, and shaped no expectations. She never had "company," and there was none in prospect. And yet the grave face grew graver as she bent over it, and a tender dreaminess came into her eyes. Unconsciously, even to herself, she was thinking far ahead into the future; not grasping its possibilities by any means, but simply wondering if it would contain any. Unconsciously she sighed as she laid down the robe, and thoughtfully walked from the room.

When she was gone, Tom and Anna returned to
the sitting-room; and it now being deserted, he
took the rocker, and she nestled down in his arms.

"Darling, can you realize that this is the last
night you are to visit me?" she asked.

"No, pet, I cannot. I have tried to think all
the evening that this is the last time I am to leave
you, that to-morrow we are to be united forever;
but I cannot grasp it. It all seems a dream to me.
I've looked forward to it so much, I've pictured it
so often, that I cannot realize that the reality is
here, — that the eve of our marriage has actually
come. But it *is* here. This is the last night I am
to go away from you. No more ' good-nights;'
and no more long, cold, cheerless walks, every step
a torture because it was taking me from this para-
dise. Thank heaven, it is all over with! and to-
morrow I shall take you to myself forever more,
my beautiful, beautiful darling!"

"And has it been so hard for you to go away
from me nights, darling?"

"Has it? Can you ask such a question, pet?"

"I know, Tom; but don't you think it has been
hard for me to have you go?"

"I suppose it was, dear one; but it never
seemed so."

"Well, it has been very hard to bear. But it
don't make any difference now: does it, Tom?
This is the last night we shall be separated. To-
morrow night, darling, you will be" —

She stopped, and buried her face in his neck.

"I will be what, darling?"

She placed her lips to his ear, and drew her arms tighter about his neck. All the love in her heart freighted the whisper, —

"MY HUSBAND."

CHAPTER XI.

AT LAST.

THE wedding-day dawned as bright and clear as is possible for a day in winter to be. The snow covered the earth, and it glistened in the rays of the sun. The air was warm for the season, — so warm, that the snow crystallized in the fields, and melted in the streets.

Tom Griggs' trunk (the circumstances of the twain permitted but one), with his own garments packed in it, was sent at an early hour to the Bayard mansion to receive Anna's clothes. Tom felt such a delightful sensation in the fact that her clothes were to lie next to his in *his* trunk! It gave him the proud sense of possession that nothing else short of the marriage-tie could give.

It was a very nervous day for Tom; but he got through with the duties of the morning all right, although it was within a half-hour of performing the service when he arrived at the house in a hack. He had a new suit of clothes throughout, but he did not look impressive. Grooms never do: that is reserved for the bride.

The home of his Anna had taken on a strange

appearance. Every thing was in a state of change. Bustle was everywhere apparent, and nothing seemed settled or natural. He was aware of being quite pale and ill at ease himself. Somehow there was not that sweet, quiet, peaceful joy he had anticipated. The expected triumph was weakened by a sense of perspiration. The romance was blunted by the all-prevailing evidence of practicability.

He was shown upstairs to the front bedroom, where he found the expectant bride, her sister, and two young lady-friends. To Tom's agitated gaze this trio bore the appearance of immediate friends of the deceased. His darling was too nervous, under the excitement of preparation, to shed much love upon him. She was getting on her gloves, and adjusting a bow, and trying her skirts; and so the poor girl had hands and mind full to overflowing.

"Why, Tom, what kept you so late?" she managed to gasp.

"I couldn't help it. Every thing went wrong."

It always does.

"Is it all right behind?" she nervously asked. This was addressed to one of the young ladies, and referred to the set of her skirt. The party questioned hastened to assure her that "it was just lovely."

It certainly was. Perhaps the dear girl did not realize it, — how could she under the circumstances? — but she appeared superbly. Her shapely form was set off to the best advantage by the graceful robe. Her face, always beautiful in the cut of the features, was radiant with the happy excitement that filled her life, and the glorious eyes were ablaze with the expectant glow of the hour. As full of trepidation as was Tom Griggs, he could not help noticing her wondrous loveliness, and thanking heaven that all this radiance was his own.

There was a fidgety air upon them all, excepting, perhaps, Lucy, whose tranquil face became all the more composed as compared with those about her.

The minister had arrived, and his voice could be heard on the lower floor. This was reported by one of the young ladies, who had resolved herself into a committee of one, and had stationed herself at the head of the stair, with a hearing apparatus tuned to its highest pitch.

The moment had arrived. Mrs. Bayard, very much flustered, appeared in person to see if all was ready here, as every thing was in readiness and waiting *there*. She was dressed in a stiff, unwieldy black silk, and appeared so uncomfortable as to make Tom wince. Anna had been satisfactorily impressed with the fact that her dress could not fit better by any possibility; and now, as her mother appeared, they were fastening on her bonnet. With this done, she stood complete to travel; and as there was but little time intervening between the ceremony and the train's starting, and as they were to have a lunch, it looked very much, as Mr. Quimby himself expressed it, as if they were going to "take a bite, and run."

The announcement that the minister was waiting increased the trepidation of the twain for whom he was waiting. It was a momentous event. For ever and ever they were to be united. Was there the faintest lurking of a fear in the heart of either? No: they loved each other too devotedly for this. He knew, that, when he took her to be his wife, he was taking an angel into his life. She felt perfectly safe in giving the keeping of herself forever into his charge, to cut herself forever adrift from her home, because he loved her. There was no one on earth, or in the heaven above the earth, that she trusted as she trusted him. Nevertheless there was a solemnity in this severing of all former ties, and taking upon themselves a new tie; and, also, there was a vague sense of dreaminess in the consummation of the event to which their hopes and desires had looked, as if it could not be all real.

The mother and the two young ladies proceeded downstairs, across the hall, and into the parlor; and following them came the *two*. Her arm rested in his, and he could feel it tremble. He was powerless to strengthen her, being himself too nervous to even command his own resources; but he was very proud and very happy.

The minister rose as they entered. The friends,

grouped about the room, searchingly observed
them.   They took the position assigned them, and
the minister began the ceremony.   In five minutes
it was over.   The dream of their lives was realized :
she was his wife ; he was her husband.

"Mrs. Griggs, permit me to congratulate you,
and to wish you a long and happy wedded life."
It was her pastor who addressed her.   He was the
first to break the embarrassing silence that followed the ceremony.

Mrs. Griggs!   How simple the words ! but, ah !
how much they expressed to her !   Yes : she was
no longer Anna Bayard, courted by Tom Griggs ;
but she was now Mrs. Griggs.   It was the badge
of a new existence, the diploma of a graduated
joy.   His *wife*, with *his own name!*   In the pro-
nunciation of that simple title was revealed the
crowning of a life-hope, the fruition of an intense
desire, the fulfilment of a daily dream.

What a thrill the name brought to her ! what a
thrill it brought to him !   There was this difference
between the two, as it always has been and always
will be in loving wedded twains : to her it was a
sensation of being possessed ; to him it was the
sensation of possessing.

After the congratulations the party adjourned
to the sitting-room, "where," as the next issue of
"The Gazette" expressed it, "an ample lunch
was prepared," to which they gathered with the
best of feeling, because every one was delighted,
as every one feels in duty bound to be at a wedding.

And every one ate with a relish, and cracked jokes, and laughed, and said things that, isolated by themselves, would have been highly ridiculous, if not criminally silly, but which made more laughter. Anna blushed and laughed, and had great difficulty in keeping her veil from her face, and was afraid she would get something on her dress ; and Tom sat by her, with his face wreathed in a perpetual smile, and handled his food in a manner that very clearly indicated he was unconscious what he was putting in his mouth.

Mrs. Quimby, with a new flannel (selected especially for the happy occasion) swathing her neck, and the arnica toned down by a generous infusion of bergamot (the poor man's friend on festive events), beamed upon the company with a face all aglow with delight; while Mr. Quimby, in the fever of the general excitement, fully explained to the clergyman the intricate process by which eels are successfully bobbed for, with a few valuable hints thrown in on the best way of scaling snakes without "squoshin' 'em " in the performance.

Dockerty was there in all the glory of a green jacket with limitless buttons; and, with characteristic perseverance, conquered and completely put down seven pieces of very rich cake, and four cups of very strong coffee, — an act of devotion to the newly married couple that very nearly cost him his precious life the following night.

Mr. Phillips was there also, dressed in an array of black that was the extreme of imposing, and desiring, way down in his heart, to laugh with the loudest; but, repressing the inclination through a stern sense of what was due to his lately lacerated feelings, he devoted himself to the food instead, and with an energy that bid fair indeed to completely repair the "goneness."

The lunch completed, the carriage appeared. The treasured trunk was placed upon it, the bride and groom and Lucy and the mother within it, and two other carriages with friends followed; and thus the party proceeded to the railway-station, where the happy twain were to take their departure on the long-coveted bridal tour.

It had been Tom's ambition to have this appear to the outside world like an ordinary journey of a long-married couple, and he flattered himself that every thing was working that way to a charm. Anna did not wear the traditional white hat with the traditional long veil; and he was not dressed in that startling array of newness of exterior which he had noticed as being so conspicuous in fresh grooms. And so he took unto himself the comforting assurance that no one would suspect his and her freshness, and that much embarrassment would thereby be saved. Poor fellow! he did not realize that the blushing face of his wife, her clinging ways, her shrinking eyes, were telling the story as plainly as if all the particulars were bulletined all over her person in the very largest type; to say nothing of his own shining eyes, his nervous movements, and his overstrained, gigantic efforts to appear careless and indifferent.

But, for all this, it was a blissful journey. He pointed out all objects of interest to her, and did it with a delight that was manifest in every vibration of his voice. And then, when the day advanced, and she grew tired, she rested her head upon his shoulder with such a precious sense of rest, and he clasped her hand in one of his, and put the other arm about her; and the cars glided on, and they two whispered softly to each other, and were blissfully, blissfully happy.

Would the dream ever end?

CHAPTER XII.

MR. PHILLIPS SAVES THE OFFICE.

THE employees of "The Gallowhill Gazette" were at the station to see the young couple off, and made the characteristic remarks among men on such an occasion.

"What did you think of it, old cock?" convivially observed Mr. Phillips, slapping Redner on the back, as they walked from the station.

"It passed off very nicely, I imagine," said the young man.

"You bet it did! She was a beauty, wasn't she? I wouldn't mind being in Griggs' shoes myself. By Judas! didn't she show off stunning?" Mr. Phillips smacked his lips, and suddenly assumed a grave expression, as if he was deeply impressed by the circumstance.

At this juncture the party, consisting of the office-hands, reached the hotel.

"Hold on, fellers!" he cried. "The boss wanted me to stand treat for you, and here's just the place to do it. Come in."

Without further ado, Mr. Phillips started inside, followed readily by his companions.

Ezekiah had received, as he intimated, an injunction from Tom to treat his fellow-workmen, and had been given five dollars for that purpose. Five dollars' worth of drink dispensed to two men and a boy would, he reasoned, so unfit them for their duties, that the office-work must necessarily run behind. He was too conscientious an agent to permit this; so he discreetly maintained silence upon the amount of the appropriation, and resolved that two rounds were amply sufficient for the occasion, and the balance he would devote in the evening to several boon companions, who, not being in any way connected with the office, could not by any means endanger its interests, however full they might get. With this laudable conclusion reached, he walked up to the bar, and cheerfully observed, —

"What will it be, boys? Mine is cider-brandy."

"I guess I'll take a little Santa Cruz," said Hazelton in the subdued voice of a regular practitioner.

"Give me a bourbon straight," ordered young Goodwin in a tone of swagger.

Redner said he would take a piece of pie and a glass of soda-water.

"Lippy" called for a glass of ale.

The refreshments being disposed of after an appropriate introductory remark from Mr. Phillips, that gentleman recklessly enunciated, —

"Fill 'em up again."

This was done, and the contents speedily transferred to their several destinies.

Mr. Phillips, feeling that the desire of his employer had been judiciously carried out, returned to the office, while the others went to dinner.

About nine o'clock that night Mr. Phillips, four congenial friends, a package of cigars, and an apparently unlimited supply of cider-brandy, occupied the office of "The Gazette."

At two A.M. the moon, looking in at one of the windows, saw the form of the foreman of "The Gazette" prostrate on the floor, with his head, propped up by a pile of paper that his friends had thoughtfully arranged for him. For some time the full face of the moon peered in upon this spectacle; but the object of the attention knew nought of it. With his mouth well opened, he slumbered, the guttural sounds arising from his throat filling the deserted room with strange noises.

At five A.M. Mr. Phillips opened his eyes, and gave a start. For a moment there was a dreadfully confused condition of mind, in which he realized nothing but the fact that it was quite dark. The next moment came the consciousness that he was lying down; but *where?* If on his own bed, how did he come there? He had no recollection of going home. He had no recollection of any thing but smoke and drink and boisterous merriment, — and after that a blank. Into this blank he could not advance a single inch. He rose on his elbow, and rubbed his eyes. The action cleared his mind somewhat, and the recruited eyes saw the dim light coming in at the windows; and then Mr. Phillips comprehended the situation in all its stirring details, and with a groan he sank back on his pillow of papers. For another moment he gave himself up fully to the wretchedness of his feelings. Then he rose up to a sitting posture. His head felt very much as if the upper part of the skull had been split clear around. His mouth was parched, his tongue swollen, his throat utterly dried up.

He took hold of his head with both hands tightly, as if to keep the upper part from coming off. How horribly it ached! Alternate flashes of heat and cold shot over his frame. Mr. Phillips thought there never had existed so horrible a condition as this. He got up on his feet, shivering until his teeth chattered. The instant he assumed an erect position the room began to tilt up at one side, and then started to turn around with him. It was only by clutching a post with a desperate grip that he saved himself from being thrown. Thus holding on, he shut his eyes, and for a moment let things swim. Then he opened them again, but hung to the post; and the location of his goneness quivered under a sensation of deathly sickness.

He tried to think what he had been doing through the carousal, and at the same time strove with all his might to keep the subject from his harrowed mind. He recollected having said with great distinctness and much feeling, three several times, —

"Ain't this just solid happiness? No cold-water sneaks are we! Set 'em up, boys! Whoop!"

Oh, how he cursed himself for the utterance, and prayed that the dreadful words might die out of his memory forever! But they would not. They shot into his mind through every lull, how-ever brief, in the memories and fancies and horrors that crowded upon him; and every time they came to him he groaned aloud. Weak, trembling, and half-crazed by remorse, he found his way to the water-pipe, and helped himself freely to the liquid which but a few hours before he declared with vehemence to be fit only for babes and old women. For a moment this draught revived him, in which he began to hope that things were not really so bad as his parched system had believed them to be. If he had not been out on the street during the unconscious part of the carousal, making an ass of himself, — the reflection caused him to shiver, — he might face the affair out with his companions.

Where were they? How drunk had they been? — too drunk to have noted his calamity? or too much so to care to compromise themselves by "blowing" on him? Perhaps so. He began to take courage. But, if they had been overpowered to that degree, how could they have got away from the office while he was left prostrate? He groaned as this prop weakened. Then, too, he thought of his position on the floor, and the improvised pillow of papers, which arrangement showed intelligent action on their part. And when this fully revealed itself, and the re-action from the draught of water set in, Mr. Phillips grew deathly sick.

Then came trooping through his inflamed mind recollections of the boasts he had made, and the speeches he had uttered, and the songs he had sung during the convivial hours. They rose up in dazzling contrast to his present awful humiliation, and he cursed aloud his "brilliancy (?)" Again he applied himself to the water-pipe; but his chilled stomach refused to rally, while the pain in his head grew more dense. How heartily he despised himself! How thoroughly debased he appeared in his own eyes! How sincerely he cursed himself for ever touching a drop of the infernal stuff!

Then came another phase to the troop of thoughts, in which hope made a desperate struggle for the mastery. He would pretend to his late companions, when he met them (here he shivered, and hope very nearly went under), that he had been "playing off" all the while, and knew when they left just as well as they knew it themselves. To this end he brought his scattered wits to bear upon the case, that he might recall something that was done at the time of breaking up; but they were poor, feeble wits at the best, and, exercise them as he might, he could not get them beyond a certain point in the carnival. All after that was a blank, the more frightful because of its hidden possibilities. What awful folly had he been guilty of during that period ? His inflamed imagination pictured the height of silliness as filling it, and he shivered even while the perspiration broke through his fevered skin.

He lighted the gas, — his hand trembling so, he could scarcely hold the match, — and looked shrinkingly about the room.   There were still standing the boards on which the spread had been made. On this table stood some shreds of bologna, a lot of broken crackers, several cigar-stumps, a bottle, and two glasses.   At the sight of each of these eloquent reminders of his folly he groaned afresh. He looked on the floor, and saw the wreck of two other tumblers, and two more bottles, and other reminiscences of the colossal shame.

He was obliged to gather them up, although every downward motion sent the pain surging in waves of agony to above his eyes.   But he hastened to clear away the vestiges ; for in a little while people would be stirring on the street and at the house, and he wanted to get home unobserved.   All the while he was doing this his mind was on the rack in its effort to recall the events of the preceding evening, and to strive to pierce the veil between memory and the awakening.   He shrank with a sickening sensation from each resurrected horror ; yet the subject possessed a fascination that he could not resist.

The last memory of the affair that he could clutch was hearing the clock strike twelve, and some one suggest that they had better break up.

He could not identify this person; but he recollected that he had two heads, and that, on the suggestion being made, he himself had jumped up,
and smitten the table with great feeling, and had
vehemently cried, —

"Not by a damn sight! We won't go home till
morning, brothers. Set 'em up! Hoop-la!"

At the recollection of this dreadful speech, the
natural solemnity of Mr. Phillips' face intensified
to a degree that was simply appalling. His great
eyes, now bloodshot, rolled hysterically in their
sockets; and his long, drooping nose showed the
clearest disposition to dive into his bosom, and
take refuge under his vest.

"I never shall touch another drop of liquor as
long as I live!" he cried in a frenzy of remorse.
"*Never*, NEVER, NEVER!" he reiterated with
increased vehemence.

Then he turned out the gas, and took his shivering frame and demoralized system and splitting
head to his boarding-house. This and his room
he reached without being seen by anybody. The
room was very dark and very cold: the former he
relieved by lighting a lamp; but from the latter
there was no relief, except by going to bed. This
he did not dare do, for fear that his slumber would
be heavy, and carry him well into the forenoon.
He had a presentiment that one or more of his
late companions would be at the office early to see
about him, and he wanted to be there to show that
he was not so overcome as they imagined him to
be. He would not — he *must* not — miss that.

Then there was another reason why he should keep awake. He had been directed by his chief to attend a political convention in a neighboring town the following day, and would have to go to-day to be there at the caucus in the evening. He was in no condition to do this. A funeral or an execution would have been more in his line, were he able to report any thing in his frightfully demoralized state. He determined to send Redner in his stead; and he must see him early, as the only available train for this place left Gallowhill at ten A.M.

So he sat on the bed, and pulled the clothes around him, and waited until he heard Redner, who occupied the next room, getting up.

Then he went in there, and told him what to do, with directions how to do it. This done, Ezekiah returned to his own room, emptied the water-pitcher into his feverish throat, arranged his toilet, and went downstairs to wrestle with a cup of coffee.

CHAPTER XIII.

REDNER WRITES A LETTER.

IT was a long ride, and to the ordinary traveller it was a tedious one; but Redner had armed himself with copies of "The Ledger," "Weekly," and "Saturday Night;" and with this array of palatable nourishment he was well fortified against weariness. Besides, the novelty of the mission, and the prospect of writing something that was to go into print, were in themselves sufficient to lift his mind to a plane far above that pursued by a railroad. So Redner buried himself in the fortunes and misfortunes of the several heroes and heroines, and saw a George Redner in every one of the former, and a quiet-faced, blue-eyed girl in every one of the latter.

He was scarcely aware that any time had passed, when the four-hours' ride was over, and he was at his destination. He found his way to a hotel, and saw, on reaching it, that most of the delegates were stopping there. He got a room and his dinner, and then went down into the office and the reading and bar rooms, moving about among the men there assembled, and listening to what they said.

He found men in pairs or groups at every step.
Some were talking loud; others in low, confidential whispers.   Although young in years, and new
to this business, he did not fail to notice that
these men wore an incongruous appearance.   They
looked like muffled drums, or Shakers in plaid
pants, or a seal-skin sacque on a lawn dress.   They
were, for the most part, tawny-haired and tawny-
bearded men, dressed in black, and stiff in movement.   When one was not awkward, he was fop-
pish to a degree that was offensive.   He tried
to associate these uncomfortably rigged people
with their homes and their home pursuits, but
fell back from the task defeated and chagrined.

The short, thin man, looking fully ten years
older than he really was, with a stoop to his
shoulders, and long white hairs on the back of
his hands, he strove to picture following a plough,
or pitching hay, or foddering cattle; and then he
looked at the shiny black suit, and sighed.   A
burly man, with nobs on his hands, and short, flat,
broken, begrimed nails at the ends of his fingers,
he was anxious to believe was a mechanic, and he
tried to put him alongside of a bench in a dusty
shop; but he looked at the shiny black suit, and
sighed again.

It was a painful spectacle, and depressed the
spirits of the young reporter.   He grew tired of
wandering among these men, whose faces were as
strange as their appearance was incongruous.   He
grew tired of the catarrhal manifestations, the

elevated feet, the loud guffaws. He was preparing to go out on the street, when he was touched on the arm by a short, stubby man, dressed in coarse clothes, and wearing a rather broken and rusty fur cap. The face was as strange as the rest to Redner, and was a very freckled face, with large, colorless eyes.

"I hope you'll excuse my speaking to you, sir," said the owner of these features; "but ain't you the gentleman that writes for 'The Gallowhill Gazette'?"

"I am," said the young man, with unction.

"I'm from Gallowhill, myself," volunteered the man. This was not said in a tone of sympathy, but rather of congratulation.

"Are you?" said Redner indifferently.

"Yes, sir. I have been to work here cutting stone for the past six weeks. You never seen me in Gallowhill, I guess."

"No."

"How's Mr. Griggs? He's to be married soon, ain't he?"

"He was married yesterday." Redner said this rather stiffly, as he could not understand what business it was to the man.

"Yesterday, was it? Well, I declare! I knowed he was a-going to be married afore I come away; but I didn't know when, though. An' so it was yesterday, hey? Well, I guess my old woman had her hands full."

"Your wife?" suggested Redner, wondering

what she could have had to do with the ceremony,
yet glad that he stood and talked with the husband of one who had been under the same roof
with Lucy.

"Yes: she washes for Mrs. Bayard, and helps
'em when they have any thing going on. I got a
letter from her the other day, an' she said the wedding was a-coming off putty soon, an' she would
have to be there a couple of days or so to help
'em. Maybe you have seen her there, or heard
them speak of her. Her name is Martha Ting."

Redner explained that he had been in Gallowhill but a few weeks, and had not visited the
Bayards.

The man paused a moment, and looked uneasily
about the room. When he spoke again, it was hesitatingly: "I thought, sir, I'd like to ask you for a
favor, if you've a mind."

"A favor, eh?" said the young man. "What
is it?"

"I wanted to ask you if you'd mind doing up a
short letter for me to the old woman. You see,
sir, I ain't much of a hand at such business; an'
with the working in the stone my fingers is that
stiff that I couldn't well hang on to a pen, let alone
moving it straight. I'd like to let the old woman
know about how I'm a-doing here; and I thought,
when Bill in the stable told me a gentleman from
'The Gazette' was here, an' knowing that writing
is in your line, that I'd ask you to do it for me, if
you had the time. I only want a few lines, an'

I've got paper an' a envelope with me." As he concluded, he reached into an inside pocket of his jacket for the articles in question.

While the man was speaking, Redner was busy thinking; and by the time he had finished, if not before, he saw that the writing of this letter would be followed by its delivery by himself, and that it was more than likely it would be taken to the Bayard home. He told the man to go with him to his room, and he would write the letter. Reaching there, Mr. Ting gave him the headings of the subjects he desired treated; but as there was not much of news in the humdrum life he was leading, and as everybody about him was a stranger to his wife, there was but little to make a letter of. He gave his name to be appended thereto, and sat silently by, reverently watching the movement of the pen, until the letter was finished. Then he asked Redner if he would take charge of it to Gallowhill, and have a boy leave it with Mrs. Bayard, where his wife would get it. Redner promised to attend to this; and Mr. Ting took his departure, well pleased with his agreeable amanuensis.

The next evening Redner reached Gallowhill, and went directly to the home of the Bayards with the letter. Every step of the way he fervently prayed that Lucy would come to the door. So great was this desire, and the fear she would not, that he was all of a tremor on ringing the bell. An elderly lady answered the summons. He had seen her at the railway-station when the wedding-party went off, and he knew she was the mother of the girl he had fondly hoped to meet. It was a sore disappointment; but there was nothing to do but to deliver the letter, and go on to his boarding-house.

The next morning Lucy took the letter to Mrs. Ting's house to read it to her, as that lady was not sufficiently posted in the various lines and curves of penmanship to catch their significance with the necessary promptness.

Mrs. Ting was a muscular woman, with considerable flesh on her frame, and a powerful wen on the very end of her nose, somewhat after the manner of a unicorn. This protuberance tended to give her face a more decided practical cast than the features themselves, and their expression was wholly that way. It was a red face, as was proper enough from twenty years' suspension over the steam of a wash-tub; and the eyes were without any particular expression, as was eminently natural in a washerwoman. She was glad to see Lucy.

"An' you've got a letter from the old man too?" she said. "Why, how did you get it?"

Lucy explained that it had been left at the house the night before.

"Why!" she ejaculated, turning the envelope over and over, and examining it with lively curiosity, "it's so sing'lar it would come like that. I wonder how he's getting along. The last time he wrote, he said the rheumatism was in his leg agin." She paused as she related this circumstance, and looked musingly at the address. "Read it to me, child," she presently added, "an' let's see what he's got to say for himself."

Lucy took the letter, and opened it. As she glanced over the page, there was not in her mind the faintest suggestion of what was really a fact, —that this letter was written to her, that every stroke of the pen was followed by a thought of *her*, and that all the thoughts combined formed themselves into a picture of just this scene, — her reading the letter to Mrs. Ting.

Unconscious Lucy! Unfortunate Redner!

She did not commence at once the reading of the letter, but glanced at the top of the page with a puzzled, uncertain expression. Mrs. Ting sat opposite, her hands on her knees, her sleeves rolled up, and her eyes intently fixed on Lucy.

"What's the matter, child?" she asked. "Can't you make it out?"

"Oh, yes!" said Lucy: "I can read it easily enough; but I— I—" She stopped, and flushed slightly, and glanced nervously over the top of the page at Mrs. Ting.

"No bad news, I hope," said that lady.

"Oh, no! I think not; but I will read it to you :—

"'Stepford, March 6, 1876. My dear, precious wife,'"—

"What's that?" almost screamed the wife.

Lucy looked at her in alarm. Her face was almost white, and her eyes appeared to be starting from their sockets.

"Why, Mrs. Ting! what is the matter?"

"Good gracious! matter enough, I should think. Does he really say *that?* Have you read it right?"

"Yes: that is just the way it is."

Mrs. Ting groaned.

"I was in hopes you might have made a mistake," she said despondently. She rubbed her head, and looked about in a half-dazed manner. "I've lived twenty years with Joe Ting, and borne a good 'eal, but never nothing like this."

"Why!" exclaimed Lucy in surprise: "I don't see any thing out of the way in this."

"I s'pose not," answered Mrs. Ting sadly; "but you are young yet, child, and don't see into things as one of my years does. When Joe Ting said *that*, he was drunk or crazy, — perhaps both," she added, gloomily.

"Please don't say that, Mrs. Ting," pleaded Lucy.

"I can't help it, child. It's a dreadful thing to be sprung on me in my time of life, an' worked as I have done."

Lucy was still more amazed.

Mrs. Ting shook her head slowly and dejectedly.

"To have him goin' aroun' slingin' such bosh at me! Ugh! I never gave him any encouragement to do that. I have always been a woman of sense, if I do say it; an' he'd never try to play such soft sawder on Martha Ting if he was in his right mind. He'd never do it, I can tell you. But he's got off there among a lot of drunken scalawags, an' they're leadin' him off : they're leadin' him off. Mark my words, Lucy : they're leadin' him off." The unhappy woman took up her apron, and wiped her eyes. "But go on, dear : I can bear it. Read the rest : I'll get the strength to hold up under it."

The distressed girl, scarcely comprehending the misery of her companion, renewed the reading : —

— "'I am glad of this opportunity to send you a few lines. My work is not so hard as it was at first, and I am getting better acquainted with the people about me. The rheumatism in my lower limb '" —

"Why don't the old fool say 'leg'?" interjected the bereaved wife.

— "'Is getting much better, and scarcely troubles me at all. I think I will experience no more pain from it. I sent you forty dollars by a postal order last Wednesday, and I hope you received it safely. I wish you would send me my flannel undergarments that I left at home. Don't forget it, darling.'" —

"Great heavens !" gasped the horrified listener as this endearing term struck upon her ear.

— "'I shall send you some more money next week. I have got a good boarding-place, much better than where I was before ; and I would be very happy if you were only with me, dear one.'" —

"Oh !" groaned Mrs. Ting.

— "'I miss you more than I can tell, my own.'" —

"Lucy !" suddenly demanded Mrs. Ting, "are those words in that letter?" She spoke sternly.

"Certainly they are," answered Lucy, looking up in surprise.

"He was drunk, then, when they was put on that paper. Mark my words, Lucy Bayard: that man was drunker than the drunkennest; and may Heaven save you from the shame that has come upon me this day! But go on: I can stand it. I'm strong: I sha'n't back down." She closed her lips tight together, and squared herself in a chair, as if preparing for a galvanic shock.

With a sorely troubled heart, the young girl returned to the letter : —

— "'But in a few weeks I will be with you again. Don't grieve over my absence.'" —

"Oh!" shot from the compressed lips.

— "'The time will soon pass. I count the days impatiently.'" —

"Drunk!" ejaculated the listener.

With a trembling voice, Lucy continued, —

— "'But soon they will be gone ; and then I will come to you, and take you in my arms, and kiss you again and again, my blessed wife.'" —

"Drunk as a fiddler!" groaned the wretched woman.

— "'Affectionately, your loving husband, Joseph.'"

"Is that all of it?" demanded Mrs. Ting, trying to master her grief and anger and shame.

"Yes : that is all."

She rose from her chair, took the letter into her own hands, and at once threw it into the stove.

"O Mrs. Ting!" cried Lucy, "how could you do that? It was from your husband, and I do not see why you feel so about it."

"Child," said the unhappy wife, softening in her anger as she looked into the distressed face of the lovely girl, "you are young now, as I said afore, an' don't understand; but when you are married twenty years, an' your man calls you his darling (ugh!) an' such rubbish as that, you can mark it down at once that he is drunk or crazy. No man in his sober senses would go to doin' it. It ain't nateral; it ain't human. Joe Ting was drunk when that letter was writ, — drunker than a fiddler, or he wouldn't a slobbered around like that. What he wants is to be laid over a barrel, an' pounded with a fence-rail till all that bosh an' bad rum is pounded out of him. That's what he wants; an' I hope to Heaven some one will get hold of him, an' do it before he shows his face in this house." She went back to her work, her lips tight shut, and her brow darkened.

Poor Lucy looked after her for a moment, sorely puzzled by it all; but, seeing she did not unbend from her frigidity, she returned silently to her home.

Unfortunate Redner! Happily he did not know how had been received the sentiments which had sprung spontaneously from the inner temple of his heart.

But it is more than likely, that, when Mr. Ting has occasion to have another letter written home, he will insist upon its contents being carefully read to him before sending it.

CHAPTER XIV.

IN THE NEW HOME.

THE train bearing the young married couple back from the tour reached Gallowhill Saturday evening. It was Anna's desire to return then, because the next day was Sunday; and her first appearance at home as a bride would be in her best attire, and before a much larger number of her town-people than would be possible on any other day. She had often pictured herself sweep-ing into church as a wife on the "first Sunday," the observed of all observers. It had been a dream with her long before she knew Tom Griggs, to be deepened and intensified after she became his pledged wife. Anna's wedding-silk was to be worn in Gallowhill for the first time that Sunday. It was an ashes-of-roses, exquisitely trimmed, and an admirable fit. Anna contemplated it with par-donable pride; Tom, with rapture.

They were going to begin housekeeping at once. The new home was a small structure, rented a few days before the wedding. The carpets and furniture had already been ordered, and during their absence the mother and Lucy had seen the

new place put fully to rights, and now it was
ready to receive them; but Mrs. Bayard believed
it best, as it was night when they came, that they
should go to her house for tea, and then to their
own roof. This Anna would not listen to. She
and Tom had provided every thing necessary for
an immediate occupation, and the first tea in the
new home had been the one bright picture before
them all the time of their absence. They could
not give it up now.

So they were driven directly to their own house;
and, there being a good fire in the kitchen-stove,
the work of preparing tea by the deft fingers of
Mrs. Bayard required but a few moments. Long
before Anna had looked at the things Lucy attempted to show her, the table was spread, and
the tea ready.

Of course Anna took the head of the table,
and presided; and in doing it she made a most
charming picture. Her beautiful face was flushed
by the excitement, the glad anticipation, the novelty of the scene; and her eyes shone with the
delight that was in her heart. There was just a
trifling tremor in the hand that directed the tea-
urn, and a nervousness in the anxiety to see that
all were helped. But she was so proud, so happy.
The joy that filled her life was manifest in every
move, every word, every glance; and, whenever
she turned her shining eyes upon her delighted
husband, that individual would immediately jump
up from his place, and go around to her, and take

the beautiful face right up to his own, when it
would for a moment be lost to the view of the
others.

And so, with the kisses and the laughter, and
her wanting to know what he thought of the
dishes and the cutlery and the napkins, and this
and that (although he had seen them all as much
as she had), the tea was prolonged for a full hour.
But it was such a delicious hour that no one
minded the flight of time, and all were astonished
when they looked up at the clock, and saw how
long they had been sitting there.

The mother said that she and Lucy would clear
off the table, and wash the dishes; but the young
wife would not listen to that. She was such a
wilful young wife, and was so determined to take
charge of every thing, that the mother and Lucy
gave up to her. Dear girl! she could not bear to
surrender an atom of her prerogative; but she
wanted with her own hands to do it all. Tom
opposed, because he knew she was tired from the
journey; but when she had pinned on the pretty
bib-apron Lucy's forethought had provided for
her, and pushed up her sleeves, she looked so
bewitchingly cosey and home-like that he gave up
all opposition at once, and was only too glad of
the opportunity for seeing her thus attired. Certainly his precious wife never appeared more dear
to him than she did at this moment; and he could
not resist catching her in his strong arms, and giving her one of his anaconda embraces.

"O Tom!" she laughingly cried, as she released herself, "what a sad plight you have got my new apron in! Lucy will be real mad at you for mussing her work."

But Lucy promptly repudiated such a sentiment, whereupon Tom felt warranted in taking another risk, and did so, greatly to the distress of the apron.

"Now, Lucy," she said, drawing her face down into a very demure compass, "you can help me by drying the dishes while I wash them, and Tom can entertain mother, and she can entertain him; and thus both will be kept out of mischief while we do the work. Now, Tom," she added, looking very gravely at him, and holding up a very pretty hand to enforce his attention, "you keep right there by mother, and don't you dare stir one step."

Having thus provided for him, she set to work with Lucy to clear the table. It must have been a remarkable dish-closet (although, to an ordinary mind, there was apparently nothing extraordinary about it); for, upon the storing away of every piece therein, she would impulsively exclaim, —

"O Tom! do come and look at this!" And he would straightway go and look, and immediately thereafter there would come from the door a half-smothered voice in vehement protestation: "Ooh-ooh-ooh! Oh my, you have just taken my breath! Go away, you great bear! and don't come near me again to-night."

Of course he would go away; and of course he was almost immediately called again, when the same performance, with scarcely any variation, would be repeated. Then the dishes were to be washed; and during this operation the young wife was as circumspect and dignified as a housekeeper of twenty years' standing. It was delightful to watch her movements, — at least Tom found it so: for he did not take his eyes from her a single moment; and, when she gave him a glance, it was so full of solemnity, that the happy fellow would laugh outright.

After the dishes were put away, Mrs. Bayard showed Tom the location of the coal-bin in the cellar, and Anna went down, too, to see where the vegetables were stored; and, when she saw how nicely every thing had been arranged, she just clapped her hands like a pleased child, — a manifestation which was immediately taken by her ever-watchful husband as an invitation for his attention, and the next instant she was struggling in his enthusiastic arms.

She really enjoyed seeing him shovel the scuttle full of coal. It was the first time he had done such work in years. But he did it well, and mounted the stairs with his burden with all the decorum of a full-fledged benedict, greatly to the amusement of Anna, and even to the relaxation of the grave face of Lucy.

When upstairs again, Mrs. Bayard gave Anna some advice in the matter of preparing breakfast;

and, it then being late, she and Lucy took their departure. Anna dearly loved her mother and sister; but she was glad when they were gone. She wanted to be alone with her husband, to go with him through all their rooms, to talk with him of the joy in their lives. And so she and Tom went through the house together.

It was not much of a journey; for the twain were in humble circumstances: but every step of the way was a sweet sensation; and, better than all, what they had was so all-sufficient, that not a thought came into their minds of how much better and how much more extensive their goods would have been had there been more money in the purchase.

And, when they came back to the sitting-room, he drew the easy-chair to the fire; and she sat on his knee, and put her arms about his neck, and laid her face close to his, and softly cried.

He did not say any thing to her. He knew that she was too happy to find expression in any other way but this: so he drew her a trifle closer in his arms, and kept silent, while her tears flowed freely.

By and by the intensity of her feelings became subdued, and the tears grew less and less; but she did not speak. She did not care to speak. All she cared was to lie there close to him, and feel his arms about her, and his face against her own. Every dream of her loving nature, every picture of her bright fancy, was realized in full; and the joy that filled her life found its truest expression in her silent tears.

And thus these two, strong in their love, happy in the present, and full of precious trust in the future, rested together in their new home in perfect peace.

CHAPTER XV.

MR. PHILLIPS DISTINGUISHES HIMSELF.

THE week following the return of Tom and Anna, they joined a skating-party. It was well on in the month of February, and the skating would soon be over: so it was arranged to have the party then. It was a delightful night, and the ice was in fair condition. The party were young, full of animal spirits, and comparatively free from care; and thus every thing was favorable to a season of enjoyment. Among the number was Mr. Phillips, who had not been on skates for some time, but who modestly admitted, that, when a boy, he "could skate the legs off of Jupiter," — a performance whose detail he did not explain, but which must have required, as was readily inferred, no small amount of skill. Mr. Phillips, on this occasion, escorted a dressmaker, who occupied a room nearly opposite his boarding-place. Having been three days in the employ of Mrs. Quimby, she had been brought under his immediate notice; and, with that gallantry which characterized him, he had paid her the high compliment of bestowing the full treasure of his heart upon her.

The ice was reached in safety. It was in a
basin, fringed about the shores with pines and
hemlocks, like sombre hackmen waiting for an
audience to disperse. The ice lay in a glittering
sheet under the beams of the moon. A dozen or
more of young people were flying over the surface,
with occasionally one here and there abruptly
sitting down upon it.

Mr. Phillips, with his usual forethought, ripped
a board from a fence near at hand for the ladies
to sit upon while having their skates adjusted.
Tom held his darling in his lap, and put on her
skates very much as he would pull on a pair of
boots. When the happy girl saw all the other
heads down, she would bring her pretty lips suddenly against his. She was very happy.

In the mean time Mr. Phillips was distinguishing
himself in his own peculiar way. The legs of
Jupiter which he had once been able to skate
completely off grew so colossal by the time he
reached the ice, that he began to doubt very seriously if he had ever been able to affect them at
all, let alone disposing of them entirely. The
dressmaker, whose name was Miss Blivens, was in
a state of great excitement. She was a novice on
skates, and was very much afraid she would fall,
and hurt herself. She gave expression to this
belief about forty times while the gallant Ezekiah
was adjusting her skates. It was not so often,
however, that he failed a single time to respond in
a tenderly assuring manner that there was not the

faintest danger of her falling — with him at her side. He was even grieved that she should entertain such a fear. Club-skates, with screw and clamp fastening, were a novel feature in that line to him. The last skating he had done was with the strap article. He saw that the club skate was a more convenient article, and he could not help deducing therefrom that it was a much better article to get around on.

With Miss Blivens provided for, Mr. Phillips proceeded to put on his own skates; and, this done, he got up, and helped her up. Mr. Phillips anticipated an abundance of bliss from this night's venture. He saw, with that keenness of perception peculiarly developed in him, that she was a superior being, — one to love, to admire, to lean upon in the hour of adversity; and his whole heart went out to her in a spontaneous burst. Looking into her face, he could not understand how it was that he ever should think he loved any one else. It *was* odd. And now he was to skim over the glittering ice with her for hours.

They made a delightful picture as he helped her up to her feet. He held both of her hands for that purpose, while his feet wobbled on the skates in a manner that looked very much as if he did not have perfect control over them. There was a smile on his face; but the look of intense anxiety that lay over it robbed it of all significance. Miss Blivens had to sit down again while he tightened his skates. This done, she was helped up once

more, and he proceeded to feel his way out on the
pond with her.   It was very new, and very exciting, and withal very delightful to Miss Blivens.
She clung tightly to his hand with one of hers,
and with the other she hung desperately to his
sleeve.   It was delightful to him to have her thus
cling, and to hear her little nervous exclamations,
" O Mr. Phillips ! don't let me fall."

Let her fall !   He might permit the eternal hills
to fall, or even stand impassively by while the
whole universe went over in a disastrous heap.
But she ! never !

Still, with this beautiful sentiment thrilling his
breast, there was a vague sense of uneasiness
back of all.   He kept on his feet, but the skates
acted curiously.   He simply wobbled along ; and
the movement was not only ungraceful, but it
threatened to wrench him apart at the hips.
Besides, there was a lively sensation of going over
backwards, to resist which strained every nerve.

She was very timid, and very fearful of falling ;
but he spoke soothingly.

" There is no danger, Miss Blivens, — none in
the least.   Just keep up straight, and hang on to
me, and I'll keep you up."

" I know, Mr. Phillips ; but then, you see, I've
never been much on skates, and I feel so frightened.   But you have had so much experience, that
you forget how a new beginner feels."

" Well, that's so.   There's something in that,"
said Mr. Phillips, straightening himself proudly.

There was a great deal in it. It was the most graceful tribute a woman can pay to a man. Her sharp eyes had detected at once his perfect control of himself on the ice. Mr. Phillips was highly gratified.

"Oh! you'll make a splendid skater yet, Miss Blivens," he cheerfully assured her. "You've got it in you, I know. It's nothing when you get used to it. All you've got to do is to do just as you see me do. You see, in the first place, you want confidence. You don't want to think of falling at all. You want to believe you are going to do it, and then you'll be sure to do it." Mr. Phillips smiled blandly over the safe deliverance of this information.

"Is that the way, Mr. Phillips?" she tremulously asked, clinging to him so helplessly that he was thrilled to the very marrow.

"That's the very way, my — ahem!" He was going to say "dear," but rescued himself from the temerity by a mighty spasm, and blushingly substituted "friend."

However, he compensated himself for the loss by bestowing on the top of her head, which was directly under the protecting range of his nose, a glance of infinite tenderness.

They wobbled along a few steps farther.

"Are you enjoying it, Miss Blivens?" he thoughtfully inquired.

"Very much, Mr. Phillips," she was good enough to say.

"It is so exhilarating," he rejoined. They were moving ahead at the somewhat startling speed of a mile an hour. "There's nothing like it to start up the blood. It makes one feel like a new person. When I'm on the ice like this, and the moonlight is falling, and the cries of the other skaters fill the air, and I'm skimming over — Ooh! ah! Take care! Great Judas!"

The awful suddenness with which Mr. Phillips' legs flew out from under him wrenched this exclamation from his pallid lips in a half-scream. It was so incomprehensibly sudden, there was no time to catch hold of any thing, or to think. In a flash he was on his back, striking the ice with a force that knocked the breath clean out of his body, and dragging the unfortunate Miss Blivens over with him in a confused whirl of elaborate dress-goods. Fortunately, in her descent, one of her skate-heels rasped him back of the ear, and the shock restored him to consciousness. At the same time a skater was passing near at hand; and by his timely aid Miss Blivens was lifted to her feet, and sustained until Mr. Phillips could perform the same office for himself. Then he clasped her hand, and she again clung to his sleeve. But it was almost a mechanical motion on his part. Mr. Phillips was very much subdued.

"O Mr. Phillips! how did it happen?" gasped Miss Blivens, very much shaken up herself by the dreadful suddenness of the affair, and somewhat troubled by suspicions of her appearance in the descent.

Mr. Phillips was not quite positive as to the cause of the mishap; but he had an impression that some unprincipled person had dropped grease on the ice, and even spoke sternly of a nature that would be guilty of such an act.

The conversation was not resumed where it was broken off by the accident. For the present, Mr. Phillips' thoughts were bent on the ice, for which he was beginning to cherish a feeling of profound awe. It was well he was thus occupied; as, otherwise, the wobbling motion he was obliged to make, and the helplessness of his lady, might have eventually become a tiresome performance. For a few minutes they squirmed over the ice in unbroken silence. Near them was a small island of bogs, with high tufts of grass springing therefrom. It was free of snow. Mr. Phillips, perceiving this, steered their course in its direction. The moment he saw the little island, he evolved a plan for immediate action.

He felt that the woman who was clinging so convulsively to him, and threatening every moment to throw him over on his head again, was one designed to make his life happy, and without whom it would be useless to attempt to live. Thoroughly convinced of this, it was natural that he should seek to learn if she felt correspondingly toward him. He could not do this as they were; for a sudden slip might not only jeopardize his suit, but his limbs or skull as well. He thought it best to secure her by a seat on one of the bogs, and thus unhampered he would skim around on the ice to show her his skill; and, having warmed her up to a high pitch of enthusiasm, he would take a seat by her side, hold her hand with a gentle pressure, and pour into her ear the story of his great love. This was what Mr. Phillips denominated "striking the iron while it was hot."

Getting her seated was a matter of great difficulty, owing to the perverse nature of the ice and their skates; but he finally succeeded in performing it, although not in a very graceful manner. Miss Blivens was glad indeed to sit down, after the strain she had been subjected to in keeping her feet.

Mr. Phillips now set about to show her what he could do on skates.

The first shove out of his foot warned him that he must use more caution, or he would skate himself apart. He was surprised to see how readily his foot moved when it started. It was only by a powerful wrench that he succeeded in recovering it, and saving himself from going over. The shock sobered him. With much greater care he began again, but it was difficult work. He found that it required considerable effort to maintain a perpendicular, and it was only by short strokes that he was able to keep up. This undoubtedly came from lack of practice. He moved around in this way for about five minutes, to use himself to the motion, and then he grew a trifle more venturesome. He saw, that, as long as he kept his feet going, he was all right. He presently detected, also, that it was much easier to keep them going than it was to make them stop. He discovered this after twice wrenching his back so seriously as to fill him with dire alarm about the ultimate safety of his spine. He noticed, too, that turning around seemed to require almost as much management as the manœuvring of forty thousand troops in the presence of a vindictive enemy.

He had got away some little distance from the anxious lady watching him, when he determined he would bear down upon her with full speed, just to show her how he could do it, and then take a seat at her side, and learn his fate. He felt that success in his suit depended in a measure on the way he acquitted himself, — the impression he made on the very eve of his proposal. It was a critical stage in his life, and he appreciated it keenly. He wanted to sail up to her erect and graceful, and to that purpose he now concentrated every thought and muscle. Getting himself faced about by a sort of jig motion (entirely beyond his control), so as to face her direction, he slapped his treacherous stomach with the injunction to "brace up," and started.

He put every muscle and nerve into play; and, while his plunges were somewhat spasmodic, still he made excellent speed. When he got within ten yards of her, he brought both feet together, straightened his body, folded his arms across his chest, and sailed forward in pleasing style. At five yards of her a bright thought struck him. He would spread out his feet, and then whirl suddenly around, thereby cutting the well-known and exceedingly pretty design called the "spread eagle." He had done it a thousand times when a boy, and remembered just how to make it. With this view, he cried to her, "See here, Miss Blivens!" And then he spread his feet.

The instant he did so he saw the dreadful mistake he had committed. His feet passed immediately beyond his control, and went apart so far as to threaten to split his body in twain. He made a desperate clutch to recover them, caught one, made a grab for the other, threw out both arms wildly for support, quivered for just one instant in the air, and then went down on the back of his head with awful velocity, and with an expression on his face that defies all description.

Miss Blivens screamed outright.

The force of the blow caused a million lights to dance before his eyes. Then there was a moment of darkness, and Mr. Phillips came back to this life to discover that he was sitting on the ice, and that Tom Griggs was putting on his hat. He made no answer to the inquiry if he was hurt. As every nerve in his body was testifying most eloquently to the general wreck of his structure, he perhaps thought any testimony from his lips would be superfluous. There was a terrible ringing in his head that tended to confuse his ideas of what had taken place. He sat there, and stared vacantly ahead of him, the awful solemnity of his features being beyond all description.

His eyes fell upon the skates on his feet. A tremor convulsed his frame.

"Take off those devilish things," he said.

The request was complied with, and he was then assisted to his feet.

His lower limbs felt as if they had been wrenched from their sockets, and put back wrong; his spine was a solid mass of ache from its base to his neck; his coat was split the full length of its back; and his head was full of ringing noises, as if its contents had hardened into metallic substances, became detached, and were rattling around loose. So strong was this latter impression, that he refused to move his head, for fear of mixing the particles in irretrievable confusion.

He did not take a seat by the side of Miss Blivens, and pour into her ear the story of his passionate love. He did not even look for her, or ask after her. It was most extraordinary, but he really hoped he would never see or hear of her again. A complete revulsion of feeling had set in. He was convinced that she was the sole cause of his mishap. If he had never seen her, he would not have been in this plight. As it was, he was undoubtedly battered beyond all hope of repair, and would forever after carry through life a patched-up and very much dilapidated carcass. He felt so intensely on this point, that when Anna innocently observed, "Poor Miss Blivens! she was terribly frightened," he savagely muttered, —

"Dammer!"

CHAPTER XVI.

IN WHICH ONE OF THE CHARACTERS FADES AWAY.

THE new journeyman from Boston did not wear well in the office of "The Gazette." He was too slow at the case to suit Mr. Phillips in times of emergency, when what type was not set by the force had to be made up by himself. We all can understand this feeling. He was too imperfect in his work first, and in his proof-correcting next, to please Tom Griggs. He was guilty of the most absurd errors in type, which were frequently perpetuated in the paper through his carelessness in dealing with the proofs. His deficiency in the art preservative caused Hazelton to look upon him with an unfriendly eye; while his long hair, cloak, and disinclination to go on sprees, were deemed by Goodwin and "Lippy" sufficient ground for their dislike.

Redner was aware he was not congenial to the human particles of the office; but he understood that it was because he was on a plane infinitely above them, and he punished their action by keeping more to himself. In this isolation it was natural he should seek for sympathy. One of his intensely sentimental nature could not possibly tie up love within himself: it must go out to some object. His went out to the sweet-faced Lucy Bayard.

His opportunities for seeing her were not frequent; but he held her constantly in his thoughts, and subscribed for two more literary papers, and walked by her home as often as was possible. He also regularly attended the church to which she belonged, and twice had the rather delirious pleasure of walking home with her. There was nothing in his manner to awaken the divine passion in her guileless breast; but her gentle heart was touched by his isolated position, and she dealt kindly with him whenever he came in her way.

One Sunday evening, a few weeks after the skating carnival, Redner accompanied her to church. He had made up his mind on that very day to tell her of his love, and to learn from her lips if she returned the passion. That she did so he could not very well doubt; for had she not acted pleased to see him?

At the church they found Anna in the pew; and after the service she asked them to walk home with her, as she felt timid. Lucy did not ask why Tom was not with her, because Tom did not go to church often since his marriage. He liked his ease and his pipe too much after the week's work was over to dress up and go out. So the two accompanied her home. They declined the invitation to go in, — at least Redner said it was getting late, and Lucy acted on the hint thus given.

Shortly after they reached Lucy's home, Mr. and Mrs. Bayard retired, and the young folks were left alone. Redner picked up that great social lever, the family album, and turned over its exciting pages. He was on the edge of a mighty revelation, and his hand shook as he turned the leaves.

"Miss Bayard," he presently said, speaking her name with some difficulty, "I have got something I want to tell you. I hope you will not be offended with it."

Lucy said she was sure he would not say any thing to offend her, but did not ask him what it was. This rather disconcerted him. It was full a minute before he resumed, —

"I don't want to offend you. I would kill myself before I would say a word to hurt you. But I must tell you what is on my mind. You won't be angry with me?"

Lucy could not conjecture what this matter was; but she assured him she would not be angry.

"It has been on my heart a long time, — ever since I first saw you, and I cannot keep it to myself any longer. O Lucy, Lucy!" he passionately cried, suddenly dropping on his knees at her feet, and clasping his hands over his heart, while his eyes turned up so that little but the whites were visible, "I love you" —

"Mr. Redner!" cried the shocked girl, "don't do this! Don't do it!" She attempted to rise, her face scarlet with confusion; but he clutched her dress, and prevented her.

"Don't leave me!" he begged. "I love you, — love you as the herb of the field loves the dew; love you as the earth loves the gently falling rain. O Lucy! sweet Lucy" —

"Please get up, Mr. Redner! please get up!" cried the distressed girl. "You must not do this. Some one will come. Do get up!" By a great effort she freed herself from his clutch, and retired to the farther part of the room.

"Lucy," he gasped, still on his knees, with his hands stretched out to her, "don't you accept the treasure of my heart? Are you not my own?"

"O Mr. Redner! don't ask me this. Get up, please!"

"Never! till your lips pronounce my fate," he vehemently protested.

"I cannot love you, Mr. Redner," she answered, her voice trembling with the agitation of the situation and the fear of some one coming in. "Do get up, please!"

He sprang to his feet. She looked at him apprehensively.

"Miss Bayard, do you reject my suit?" he sternly demanded.

"I am so sorry," she faltered.

"Answer me."

"Don't talk of this, please! I cannot love you, Mr. Redner."

"Is all this for nought?" he tragically cried, smiting his forehead, and glaring at the ceiling. "Is my suit contemned, my love discarded?"

The poor girl was too agitated to speak.

"It is enough!" he resumed in the same tragic air, striding to the table, and putting on his hat, and fastening his cloak. "The hour will come when you will weep scalding tears over this brutal act. Ere another sun sets in yon horizon," he added, looking under the table for his cane, "my pulse will be silent in the chill mists of death."

Before she could give utterance to the horror she felt, he was gone. She sank nerveless into a chair, and pressed her hands tightly upon her eyes as·if to shut out a ghastly vision.

What should she do? what could she do? She suffered so keenly, that she could not remain still. She paced the floor in an agony of apprehension. She did not love him; she could not: but her tender heart was cruelly agonized by his suffering. Why did he ever see her? why was she ever born? She went to her room, but she could not sleep: her mind was torn and racked by a terrible fear.

On leaving her, Redner did not go directly to his boarding-house: he walked the streets for an hour, and then he went to Quimby's. Removing his shoes, he took his light, and went down to the cellar, where, finding the half of a mince-pie on a swing-shelf, he carried it to his room, and ate it in gloomy silence.

The next day he wrote her, that, if she did not change her decision of the night before, he would drown himself. She was glad to hear from him, glad to know that he was not dead. She wrote him a careful, sensible letter, gently telling him that she could not be to him what he desired, but assuring him of her esteem, and begging him to forget all about her, except as a friend. In answer to this, he wrote that he never should forget her, that she had wrecked his life, and all that remained for him now was to fade away.

In the matter of fading he was unexpectedly and materially aided the day following by Tom Griggs, who, finding an atrocious error in the paper that had been marked in Redner's proof, lost all patience, and peremptorily discharged him.

"Do you mean to tell me that you don't want me any longer?" demanded the young man excitedly.

"Yes : that is it."

"Why is this?"

"Because I can't afford to keep a man who butchers his work as you do."

"How dare you talk like that to me?" he hotly demanded.

"Here's your money," angrily rejoined Tom. "And now you leave this office at once, or I'll help you out, you miserable fraud!"

Inflamed with passion as Redner was, he could not fail to notice that Tom Griggs was fully a third larger than himself. He clutched the money, and strode to the door.

"You will hear from me again very soon," he

hissed between his clinched teeth, as he passed out.

That was three years ago, and he has not yet been heard from. But that is the way with most people : they promise to write, and then don't do it.

CHAPTER XVII.

TOM GRIGGS GETS OUT ON THE WRONG SIDE OF THE BED.

TOM GRIGGS ate his breakfast in comparative silence one Monday morning. There was a frown on his face, and he chewed his food and gulped down his coffee as if he was undergoing a most disagreeable penance. One of the selected articles in the preceding number of " The Gazette " was entitled " Cheerfulness at Meals." It .was the cream of some modern Solomon's observations on the imperative necessity of a cheerful spirit for the handmaiden to wait on good digestion. Tom Griggs reproduced the article in his columns because of its sterling sense, and it is to be hoped his readers profited by it. But Mr. Griggs was not just now thinking of this. It was the day before publication, and there was much to do to prepare the matter for that issue. To make this performance seem a mountain, and to make him feel totally unable to scale it, was the fact that he had a check out for sixty-three dollars, and not a single dollar in the bank to meet it, although it would undoubtedly be on hand itself that very day. Punctuality is the chief virtue of a check which lacks its face at its back.

The prospect of collecting the money before three o'clock was an exceedingly dismal one. So Tom chewed his food morosely, and looked at the table, and not at his wife.

It was not, perhaps, a very cheerful-looking table. It was the morning of wash-day, and the spread was doing duty for the last time. A Monday-morning table-spread is not an inspiring spectacle. The steak was considerably more than done, and was dry and hard, — very good qualities indeed in a ginger-snap. The potatoes had been left in the water after being removed from the fire, and were soggy. The coffee had been boiled too earnestly. At her best Anna was not a success in broiling steak, or making a pot of coffee; but she had a good heart and a magnificent head of hair. On this occasion she had also an aching tooth. She had been kept awake half the night by the pain; and the washerwoman was an hour late, and the wind was wrong for the draught of the stove. In the mind of the young wife there was not in all Gallowhill a more sorely tried housekeeper. Before she was married, Anna knew just how a table should be kept, the same as people outside of a newspaper-office know just how a paper should be conducted. In her case, as in theirs, experience was too much for the idea, and got away with it. She did not feel this morning as if she could lift her hand to do a stroke of work; and the ache of her tooth made her temper sore all around its edges. Absorbed in the ache, and efforts to overcome it by applications of hot coffee, she was as silent as he.

As Tom chewed his food in silence, his mind was in that condition to be easily operated upon by the least observable trifles, if of a disagreeable nature. A two-hundred-and-fifty-pound man might have wrecked his sides in an explosive guffaw right under the window without moving a single feature of Tom's face in sympathy therewith, while the whimper of a child would have almost tempted him to lift his hand in anger.

As he chewed away, his eyes rested upon the table, vaguely at first, as if his mind were engaged far distant, and then gradually concentrated on its various spots or stains, until each one grew into such significance as to seriously annoy him. This led him to recollect that the coffee was muddy, that the steak was a crisp, that the potatoes were soggy; and, recalling these little episodes, it occurred to him that the coffee was always indifferent, the steak always overdone, the potatoes always water-soaked. Once well launched on this flood of reflection, there were a number of depressing reflections ready to greet him. Was it right that things should be so? Did he not have enough to battle with, without being crippled on the start by a half-furnished stomach? It was not much to ask that his food should be cooked properly, so to get the right nourishment from it. It was not much to ask that a clean spread should deck the table the morning of the day on which he had to collect sixty-three dollars to make good a bank-account. These were such inconsiderable trifles, that he wondered why Anna did not look after them. At the same time his heart was hurt by the fact that she had not.

Thus brooding, he rose from the table; searched for his coat, and found it; searched for his hat, and found it; and then prepared to start. It was with a remarkably diffident step, as if his heart was so full of lead as to have slopped over, and run down the back of his legs, and formed a pool in each heel of his shoes. His starting aroused her. She sighed.

"Are you going?"

"Yes."

"I wish you'd step into Walker's, and tell him to send me some potatoes and a broom and a bar of soap. Tell him to send them right away, for there isn't a bit of soap in the house. And get me a bottle of camphor. I used up what mother gave me yesterday, and I can't go through another night without something to deaden the awful ache."

"Why don't you have the tooth pulled?"

"What should I do that for? It ain't a decayed tooth: it's only a cold in my jaw."

Tom knew this; but there was a certain amount of pressure on his mind that had to be let off in some way. He could not very well protest against the errand at the grocer's. Had it been possible to do so, there would have been no need to speak of the tooth. Tom wanted to assure himself, if no one else, that *she* was leaving something undone.

"What shall I get the camphor in?" he asked, the fall in his voice indicating the depth of his disappointment over the failure of the tooth as an auxiliary.

"There's the bottle mother gave me: take that. It's on the bureau," she said.

There was the shadow of an idea floating in the young husband's mind that she might have got the bottle for him, while he went after it himself. But he said nothing. Then he left the house for the office, and Anna went weariedly about the task of clearing the table, every little while stepping into the kitchen to tell Mrs. Ting about her tooth.

If Tom Griggs looked for any lightening of the cloud when out of the atmosphere of his home and in that of the office, he was not gratified. It is more than likely he had no such expectation. It is a remarkable fact in connection with the conduct of a country printing-office, that, on the day when an extraordinary financial effort is to be put forth, some mechanical or other trouble arises. A form "pies," or an important roller melts, or some one of the meagre force is unexpectedly taken sick or drunk. A short bank-account, and one, if not all, of these contingencies, invariably conjunct on the day preceding publication. People of a superstitious turn are confident there is something supernatural about this. In

the case of Tom Griggs it was the last-named
misfortune.   Hazelton, being of a frail and sickly
cast, and not expected to live any great length of
time, had gone off on a broad and comprehensive
drunk.   This fact was communicated to Tom, the
moment he entered the room, by Mr. Phillips, in
that helpless tone peculiar to the foreman of an
office when he is confronted by an emergency.
" A mighty poor look for the paper," he cheerfully
added.

Mr. Phillips' spirit communicated itself to Joe
Goodwin and " Lippy," and occasioned the former
to audibly observe, for the benefit of his employer,
" We'll be a day late, or I'm damned ! "

Whereupon Master Vanderlip was led to remark, for the behoof, also, of the dejected editor,
that, if the paper got out at all that week, it would
be mighty lucky.

The editor sat down to his desk, and groaned
inwardly, while he involuntarily clasped his head
in his hands.   Then he went at his books to
make out bills for collection.   There was an array
of uncancelled figures in the columns that were
most grateful to the casual glance, but apples of
ashes in the teeth of him who gave them a
closer inspection.   This party was out of town ;
or that one was to pay next month ; or there was
a counter-account from so-and-so ; or what's-his-
name wouldn't pay anyway : and so down one
column after another, until Tom Griggs began to
doubt if he could get bills enough for the desired

amount, saying nothing at all of what he might
collect on them. And while he was at this labor
his muddled brain was tossed and convulsed by
the cry of "copy," and the demands of visitors,
and the queries of Mr. Phillips, who never before
— so it seemed to his half-distracted chief — was
so densely helpless and ignorant as to-day. That
nothing went right became apparent before the
day had gone far. Correspondents disappointed,
"sorts" ran out, one galley was pied, and marvel-
lous stupidity seemed to settle on the compositors.
It seemed to the unhappy man as if visitors were
never half so numerous. There was a man who
had a farm to sell, and wanted fifty auction-bills.
He didn't have copy for the bill, not being used
to such things; but he knew the printer could
write it out in a jiffy. Tom complied. Next
were three women, — a committee appointed by
a church-society to get posters for a strawberry-
festival, and also to get a notice in the paper.
They had the copy for the poster, — about enough
for a small pamphlet, — and seemed to show a de-
termination to get it all on the bill in the biggest
type in the office. After a prolonged struggle
with them, he succeeded in getting their consent
to reduce the amount of matter. A full half-hour
was used up with this party. They were succeeded by a lank individual of a dim religious
aspect, and the escorter of a portmanteau. He
dealt in a line of lithographs. Tom hastily but
firmly assured him he did not want to buy, at the

same time eying him with intense dislike.   The
man said he did not want him to buy any thing:
he only wanted to show him some perfect gems of
art.   Tom told him he didn't have time to look at
them.   The proprietor of the gems assured him
it would not take a moment to see them, at the
same time opening the portmanteau, and taking
out a cluster of wares.   The victim felt like brain-
ing him, but hesitated an instant on the verge of
the act, and in that instant he was lost.   The
gems were spread out upon his desk, over the
copy, the bills, and the books, and the author of
the horror was expatiating upon their merits, while
his prey stared helplessly at the sight.   Fortunately, at this juncture, some one came in to see
about an advertisement: whereupon the agent,
with great forbearance, observed, —

"My time is not very pressing.   I'll wait until
you get through with this gentleman."

"I shall have to use this desk, and must ask
you to move your property," said Tom in desperation.   "I do not want to buy the pictures, and I
have no time to-day to look at them."

"Perhaps some of your employees would like
to avail themselves of this opportunity to secure
a few rare copies," he pleasantly suggested.

Tom shuddered.   The time of every man in the
office was precious.

"Copy," said Mr. Phillips.

The editor of "The Gallowhill Gazette" felt
that his reason was leaving him.

"There is no time to attend to you," he savagely protested, glaring at the agent. "There is not a moment to spare here all day to-day."

The owner of the gems caught up his property, and departed, very much at a loss to understand why a free and enlightened press should be cursed by a boorish management.

The half-stunned editor immediately after severally entertained the following parties : —

A man with a Western paper containing a story of a suicide which occurred several months before, and had been seen by Mr. Griggs some forty odd times. He wanted the paper saved after the article had been used, and was some time in getting away, owing to numerous injunctions to this end.

A woman with a poem, whom Tom thought to escape by telling her he would read it at another time, but ignobly failed, as the poem was an obituary to be published that week. In despair, he promised to print it, without more than a glance over its twelve verses. She said she would want five copies of the paper; and that, she supposed, would be compensation enough.

A man with a four-column newspaper article on the phenomenon of atmospherical influences on the Arizona cactus. He pronounced it the clearest and most logical exposition of this popular subject he had seen, and was very anxious to have it appear in the paper next day, Almost bereft of breath by this suggestion, Tom told him that the paper was already nearly full. The man said he was confident there wasn't any thing in it one-half as important as this, and room ought to be made for it.

A man with a written account of a visit he had made to Boston, being mostly a complimentary description of the hotel at which he had stopped, with the proprietor's name and the hotel's terms, which the article spoke of as being exceedingly reasonable. When published, he wanted a copy sent to the landlord, who would probably sub-scribe.

A man with sixty dollars' worth of advertising of a patent medicine, to be inserted for eight dol-lars ; also a five-dollar editorial, to be published in consideration of getting the contract.

A man who had taken the right of the town to sell a patent window-fixture, and came in to tell it, as he knew items of a local nature were always acceptable. Having a fixture with him, he kindly gave fifteen minutes of his time to explain its workings, and was particular to see that the half-numbed editor got his name spelled right.

A man who was an extensive grower of straw-berries for the market, and who brought in ten cents' worth of the fruit for the exclusive behoof and enjoyment of the editor, and who thoughtfully suggested, that, in case mention was made of it in the paper, it might be added that he had plenty of the article on sale.

A man who supposed the editor was glad to get any thing to fill up the paper with, and so notified him that he had a few choice cabbage-plants to sell,—a fact many of the readers would be glad to know.

This philanthropist had barely got out of the door when the shrill factory-whistles announced the hour of noon. Catching up the bills, and determined to shake the dust of the office from his feet until the bank matter was settled one way or the other, Tom Griggs started home for a hasty dinner.

The moment he got inside the house, his spirits, which had risen somewhat in the hasty transit through the open air, fell considerably in the doleful and dreary atmosphere of steam and soap. The dining-room was as he left it in the morning, excepting the table had been cleared of the break-fast-dishes, and now held a tin pail full of blueing-water, a pan of freshly wrung clothes, a clothes-stick, a pasteboard box of clothes-pins, and a partly used bar of soap.

"Gracious, Anna!" he ejaculated in dismay, "ain't you got dinner ready yet?"

"Dinner!" she returned, looking as much put out as himself. "Why, it's only twelve o'clock! and we're washing. You ought to know *that*, Tom."

"But I'm in an awful hurry, and I've got four hundred things to do this afternoon."

"I can't help it, Tom. I try to do the best I can; but I can't do every thing, and my tooth has made me half crazy: and you never said a word this morning about wanting dinner any earlier than usual. Did you get the camphor?"

"Thunder! no: I forgot all about it. But no wonder, for I've been about distracted with one thing and another. Hazelton is off on a drunk, too, to make matters worse."

"I'll get dinner now if you'll take those things off the table," she said.

"I've got no time to wait," he hastily protested. "I can eat what I want in the pantry, I suppose." And, suiting the action to the word, he helped himself to some bread and cold coffee, which he ate as if in sullen protest of his wife's tardiness; and then he left.

Anna made no remark. She wished that her husband could have had a hot dinner; but she could not believe a man who so easily forgot an errand would suffer for the want of a dinner.

Every moment of the time allotted him, Tom worked like a beaver; but, doing his very best, he could not raise the sum he required. At a quarter to three he lacked fifteen dollars of the amount. In this strait he ran across a friend, and from him he borrowed the necessary money, and got to the bank in time to make the deposit, and take up the check; pocketing the latter just as the clock struck three.

He reached the office relieved, but exhausted, and took up the burden of the coming issue of the paper.

CHAPTER XVIII.

DESTINY COLLARS MR. PHILLIPS.

In the beginning of the month of September following the opening of this chronicle, Mrs. Quimby's boarding establishment received an acquisition in the person of a widow lady. She came from the adjoining town of Sansgammon; and her mission to Gallowhill was to canvass for " Woman's Sphere," a bulky subscription volume. Her stay in the village was to extend through a period of three weeks, and during it she was to make her home with Mrs. Quimby.

She was a bustling little woman with bright gray eyes, well-filled cheeks, an easily gliding tongue, and a rather trim figure. She was most favorably disposed toward Mr. Phillips, and took every occasion to notice him. Some of the boarders, of a worldly turn of mind, attributed this attention to the fact that our friend was connected with the village paper; but Mr. Phillips entertained no such sordid thought, and, had it been suggested to him, he would have scouted it at once. A highly complimentary notice of the work, with the name of the canvasser, appeared in

" The Gazette," the copy being in the symmetrical handwriting of our gallant friend ; but it was a valuable book, and deserved, without doubt, all that was said of it.

The favor in which the widow contemplated him was very gratifying to Mr. Phillips, as well as being creditable to her powers of discrimination. With that discernment peculiar to him in the observation of female character, he was not long in discovering that she was a superior woman.

He studied her with increasing interest. He escorted her to and from church twice, and was agreeably impressed with her sensible views of pulpit oratory and theological points. He also took her to a fair and festival, and was so charmed with her qualities of mind, that he actually forgot where he was, and was relieved of eight dollars and sixty cents before recovering himself.

He had known her a period of ten days, when he became convinced, that, if he was ever to amount to any thing in this life, his future must be merged with hers.

He was passing into the sitting-room one evening, intently thinking upon this matter, when he came into her presence. She was the only occupant of the room, and she was sitting by the window to get the benefit of what breeze was stirring. When he saw that they were alone, he was very much agitated, so plainly was the hand of Providence seen in the matter.

"Good-evening, Mr. Phillips," greeted the lady,

with a smile of welcome that thrilled him to the heart's core.

"Good-evening, Mrs. Richardson," he responded in an agitated voice; for he was thinking of the opportuneness of the meeting, of the ordeal he had determined to pass through, of the array of bitter experiences that strewed the past.

"Are you not well, Mr. Phillips?" she inquired in deep solicitude.

"Oh, yes! I am well," he answered, smiling in a ghastly manner.

"You do not look well," she added, as if in doubt. "It is very warm. Perhaps the weather affects you."

"It ain't the weather," he hastened to assure her: "it is deeper than that,—deeper than that, Mrs. Richardson."

"What's deeper, Mr. Phillips?"

"The thing that's on my mind, and makes you think I ain't well, Mrs. Richardson. Do you know what I was thinking of when I came in this minute?" He gave her an enraptured glance.

"No, Mr. Phillips, I do not. What was it?" She smiled helpfully.

"I was thinking of you."

"Of *me*, Mr. Phillips? How strange that you should be thinking of *me*! And what was you thinking of in connection with me, Mr. Phillips?"

"I was thinking how much"— The foreman of "The Gazette" brought up as suddenly as if he had been shot, and shook like a leaf. He had almost precipitated himself into the dreaded vortex, without realizing that he was anywhere near it. In an instant more he would have actually done the deed; but the fate that had relentlessly pursued him for years overtook him at the very edge of the crisis, and floored him in a flash. His stomach sank; his tongue clove to the roof of his parched mouth.

Mrs. Richardson, at first startled by the unearthly appearance of his face, immediately recovered herself, and looked at him intently.

" How much what, Mr. Phillips ? "

He shook himself as if to shake off a giant, and gasped, " How much I — I — I — I — I " — He could go no farther. The last pronoun expired in his throat like the last gurgle in a pump, and he sank with a groan into a chair.

The puzzled look in her face cleared up at once. She immediately sprang into the breach.

" Do I understand, Mr. Phillips, that this 'much' refers to your regard for me ? "

" Yes," he eagerly answered.

" That your regard is very great ? "

" Yes," greedily.

" That you really love me ? "

" Yes, yes." A drowning man could not have clutched more eagerly at a plank.

" That you want to marry me ? "

" I do, I do."

"Then I am your ticket, Mr. Phillips," promptly confessed the blushing widow.

"Don't call me Mr. Phillips: call me Ez," cried the delighted man, catching her in his arms.

"EZ!"

CHAPTER XIX.

WERE THEY BILIOUS?

OF course Mr. Phillips and the happy widow had their wedding-day; but it is not our purpose to give the particulars of the ceremony. Already have we stretched this simple story beyond its contemplated dimensions, and we must bring it to a close. They were married at Quimby's. Mrs. Quimby insisted upon this; and, as the home of the fair bride in Sansgammon was but a boarding-place, she could easily consent to the proposal.

To be sure Tom and Anna were at the ceremony, although it did look at one time as if the pleasure would not be theirs. The marriage was to take place at an early hour in the day, and at nine o'clock the carriage was to call for Tom and his wife. This demanded lively action on Anna's part. She had the breakfast to get and clear away, and the other work to do, before she could dress herself. So much enforced haste made her nervous and irritable, and the temperature of her mind readily influenced him, — the two being one. Someway the cooking did not go right. It had to be in a measure slighted, of course; but the time thus saved did not appear to count much as an advantage. As soon as Tom finished eating, he proceeded to dress himself, while Anna hastened to clear away the breakfast-things. He got a clean shirt, and got it on, when he discovered that the back button was off. This was a great shock to Tom Griggs. If the crab-apple-tree in the front-yard had stepped into the room, and lifted him by his back hair, he could scarcely have been more surprised and hurt.

He took off the garment, — not, however, with that deliberation one employs in peeling a banana. Rather it seemed to come off as if by a sudden impulse. Then he threw it back of him in a manner that implied considerable agitation. He took out another shirt, and examined it hastily. It was in good condition, and he put it on. A moment later, Anna in the pantry heard her name called.

"What is it?" she cried.

"Where have you put my collars? I can't find them."

"They are in the drawer with your shirts," she answered.

There was a moment of silence.

"They ain't here," he then asserted.

Anna hastened to the room, saying, "Dear me!"

Her face fell as she saw the disordered bureau.

"O Tom! what have you been doing?" She could have cried, she was so heated and vexed.

"I have been looking for those collars, and I can't find them."

She went to the bureau.

"They ain't there," he protested.

She made no reply, but picked up several of the articles in the shirt-drawer, and brought forth a collar. It was an ungenerous thing for her to do, and Tom resented it.

"I don't see the sense, Anna, in putting my collars in a place like that, where they can't be found without burrowing like a woodchuck."

"They have always been kept there, and that is the place for them; and you would have found them if you had looked."

"Look! Didn't I look, I'd like to know?" he demanded. But she was back to her work again, without replying to him. It was not, however, because she wished to keep silent. Every moment her voice came from the other rooms in such encouraging observations as the following:—

"Oh dear me!

"I never can get ready, I know!

"Here it is nearly eight o'clock, and nothing done!

"Gracious! what shall I do?

"I sha'n't stop to make the bed.

"That carriage will be here before I've got half through!

"I'll leave the dishes in the sink until I get back."

In the mean time Tom wrestled with the collar, which refused for a long time to button; and with his stockings, that seemed determined to go on heels upward in spite of his frantic efforts to keep them down. Then he had a time of it to find his cuff-buttons, which some one had deliberately gone off with. He knew this to be a fáct, because he distinctly remembered where he put the buttons when he last used them, and they could not have walked away themselves. Some one had, undoubtedly, broken into the house in the night, and removed them. It was a contemptible trick anyway. Anna was dressing herself now, and she had too much to do to look up the buttons. But she had no sympathy with the burglar theory. If he had put the buttons where he said he did, they would be there now. He was too vexed to speak. It was so ungenerous, so harsh, for her to say this. He would find them himself, or he would go without them, before he would ask her help.

Anna was using the glass to crimp her hair. She was nervous, excited, heated. She never knew her hair to be so contrary as it was this morning; and it never had been. She burnt her hand too with the pencil. It seemed, as she admitted herself, she would go wild.

She hastily snatched a towel from the rack, and something fell on the floor. It was a pair of soiled cuffs. They were Tom's. In them were the buttons. His eyes fell on them the same time. He turned his face from her at once, and picked up the articles.

"I'd like to know who in thunder put them there," he muttered.

"It must have been the burglar," she suggested.

"I know I didn't do it," he persisted, still with his back toward her.

"Oh, it was the burglar!" she hastened to assure him. "He took the buttons, and then he hunted up the dirty cuffs, and put the buttons in them, and left them on the rack, under the towel."

"Come, Anna," he hastily said, "this is no time for foolishness."

The carriage arrived a full quarter of an hour before she was ready. This added to the flustration. He was all dressed, and, having nothing else to do, went to the front-door to look at the carriage, and then came back and told her it was there, and asked her how long she was going to be; and then went back to look at it again, and immediately returned to tell her it was still waiting, and would she never get ready. After doing this a half-dozen times, the poor girl cried out in desperation, —

"Tom, if you can't help me, for pity's sake don't drive me wild!"

He sullenly retired.

Finally she was ready. She took her handkerchief-box from a bureau-drawer to select a handkerchief. As she lifted the box, a bit of paper fell on the floor. She picked it up, gave it a hasty glance, and threw it on the bureau. He came back at this juncture, and saw the slip. As she took a farewell glance in the glass, he looked at the writing. It was brief, and in pencil. Its date was more than a year old. It simply read, —

"MY DEAR, PRECIOUS PET, — I will be up at three o'clock with a team to take you riding. I cannot bear to have you look so tired as you did last night; and so I must put aside my own work, and take you out for a while. The fresh air will do you lots of good. When we are married, darling, I won't let you get tired.

"Yours lovingly,

"TOM."

He dropped the paper suddenly, and hurried with her to the carriage.

THE BEST OF GOOD READING.

THE FALL OF DAMASCUS.

By WILLIAM WELLS RUSSELL. 12mo. Cloth, $1.50.

"In vigor of style, in freshness of thought, and in dramatic power, superior to any American novel recently issued from the press." — *Halifax (Va.) Record.*

"The author is new to us, but he has written a powerful fiction. The subject, the period, the characters, the love story sandwiched in, all conspire to make the feat difficult of success. And yet the fiction is a grand success." — *Providence Press.*

BLUFFTON.

By Rev. M. J. SAVAGE (Church of the Unity, Boston). 12mo. Cloth, $1.50.

"This novel is not a novel. It is really a controversial theologic discussion from the liberal standpoint, cast in the form of a novel. Yet it has a natural plot, and it tells an interesting story. It is written with great clearness and vigor, and is one of the most interesting books recently published. Its characters are only sketched; but they are sketched with a clear, free, and bold hand." — *Detroit Tribune.*

ROTHMELL.

By the author of "Mr. Peter Crewitt," "That Husband of Mine," "That Wife of Mine," &c. 12mo. Cloth, $1.50.

"A work of very great merit and interest, and reminds us somewhat of some of Mrs. Burnett's best productions — 'That Lass o'Lowrie's,' for example. The story, a touching one in itself, is most feelingly told, and while not in any manner overdrawn, it possesses all the elements of the highest order of romance, which is the romance of real life." — *Bancroft Messenger, San Francisco.*

SEOLA.

12mo. Cloth, $1.50.

"A strange and wonderful work of imagination." — *Indianapolis Tribune.*

"One of the most singular works ever written, being neither history nor theology, but a story founded in strict concordance with the sacred writings of the Hebrews and traditions of other nations. A work of which any one might feel proud." — *Schenectady Union.*

NOBODY'S HUSBAND.

16mo. Cloth, $1.00. Paper, 50 cents.

"Of a somewhat different kind is Nobody's Husband. It describes the adventures on railroad and steamboat of a bachelor gentleman and his friend's wife, a young lady accustomed to enjoy her own way, a baby, a dog, and an Irish servant-girl. The book is full of the author's peculiar humor, and the haps and mishaps of the party are sketched with some force." — *Toronto Monthly.*

A YEAR WORTH LIVING.

By Rev. W. M. BAKER, Author of "The New Timothy," "Mose Evans," &c. 12mo. Cloth, $1.50.

"Really a novel of merit. The characters are distinctly and artistically drawn. They become people to us fully as much as do Dickens's characters, and still are not so exaggerated. The descriptions of scenery are fine. The scourge of the South, the yellow fever, is depicted in all its horror; we know the author is acquainted with it. Take it through and through, and it is one of the most enjoyable books we have read lately." — *Indianapolis Tribune.*

Sold everywhere, and sent by mail, postpaid, on receipt of price.

LEE & SHEPARD, Publishers' . . . . Boston.

C. T. DILLINGHAM . . . . New York.

THE BEST OF AMERICAN FICTION.

A PAPER CITY.

By D. R. LOCKE (PETROLEUM V. NASBY). 12mo. Cloth, $1.50.

"We venture to say that few new books will be read with more enjoyment than this one. It is one of the finest bits of history and character-drawing ever issued from the press." — *Indianapolis Journal.*

A WOMAN'S WORD, AND HOW SHE KEPT IT.

By Miss VIRGINIA F. TOWNSEND. Author of "Only Girls," "That Queer Girl," &c. 12mo. Cloth, $1.50.

"Miss Townsend has heretofore produced many quiet and delightful home volumes; but in this new venture she soars far above her former work. There is an intensity and dramatic interest in the book that never lags, and it possesses a pure element that gives it the right tone and finish." — *Modern Argus, N.Y.*

HIS INHERITANCE.

By Miss ADELINE TRAFTON. Author of "An American Girl Abroad," "Katherine Earle," &c. 12mo. Cloth, $1.50.

"Miss Trafton, the daughter of a well-known divine, has in previous books, notably 'An American Girl Abroad,' won a reputation for lively writing of the purest type. In this, her latest venture, she is charmingly fascinating, not only in the story itself, but the manner of telling it. Pathos, humor, character, stand out in every thing connected with the heroes and heroines of the tale." — *Providence Despatch.*

AGAMENTICUS.

By E. P. TENNEY (President of Colorado College). Author of "Coronation." Square 16mo. Classic size, $1.25.

"As a study of life and character, brimful of laughter-provoking, quaint and thought-awakening surprises, for dyspeptics who cannot go to Saratoga, and intellectual people getting short of ideas, we confidently commend it as the book of the season." — *Chicago Advance.*

AN AMERICAN CONSUL ABROAD.

By SAMUEL SAMPLETON (LUIGI MONTI).

"The sixpenny way in which our consular service is managed has made it ridiculous at home and abroad: hence the troubles which beset poor Mr. Sampleton in his attempt to live within his income, and at the same time maintain the dignity of the office, are not overdrawn, and the book may do a good work. It is very readable, and interwoven with the story is a fund of information which will interest any reader who is not familiar with the consular service." — *Taunton Gazette.*

MR. PETER CREWITT.

By the author of "That Husband of Mine," "That Wife of Mine," "Rothmell," &c. 16mo. Cloth, $1.00. Paper, 50 cents.

"It is full of quaintness, abounds in humor, and is pathetic with all the rest. Our readers need no urging from us to procure this issue, as it is one of the brightest and raciest of books of its kind ever placed before the public, and is sprightly and entertaining from beginning to end." — *N. B. Standard.*

For sale by all booksellers and newsdealers, and sent by mail, postpaid, on receipt of price.

LEE & SHEPARD, Publishers . . . . Boston.

C. T. DILLINGHAM . . . . New York.

MISS AMANDA M. DOUGLAS'S NOVELS.

HOPE MILLS;
OR,
BETWEEN SWEETHEART AND FRIEND.
(IN PRESS.)

"Amanda Douglas is one of the favorite authors among American novel-readers. She writes in a free, fresh, and natural way, and her characters are never over-drawn." — *Manchester Mirror.*

FROM HAND TO MOUTH.
12mo. Cloth. $1 50

"The charm of the story is the perfectly natural and homelike air which per-vades it The young ladies are not stilted and shown off in their 'company man-ners,' but are just jolly home-girls, such as we like to find, and can find any day. There is real satisfaction in reading this book, from the fact that we can so readily 'take it home' to ourselves." — *Portland Argus.*

NELLY KINNARD'S KINGDOM.
12mo Cloth. $1 50.

The Hartford "Religious Herald" says, "This story is so fascinating, that one can hardly lay it down after taking it up."

IN TRUST;
OR,
DR. BERTRAND'S HOUSEHOLD.
12mo. Cloth. $1.50.

Miss Douglas possesses the genuine art of telling a story naturally and well. She is far removed from those sensational novelists whose prurient writings are oftenest found in the hands of the rising generation. The present story is quite fascinating, with an obvious lesson running through it, which no one can mistake.

CLAUDIA.
12mo. Cloth. $1.50.

"The plot is very dramatic, and the *dénûment* startling. Claudia, the heroine. is one of those self-sacrificing characters which it is the glory of the female sex to produce." — *Boston Journal.*

STEPHEN DANE.
12mo. Cloth. $1.50.

"This is one of this author's happiest and most successful attempts at novel-writing, for which a grateful public will applaud her." — *Herald.*

HOME NOOK;
OR,
THE CROWN OF DUTY.
12mo. Cloth. $1.50.

"An interesting story of home-life, not wanting in incident, and written in forcible and attractive style. Miss Douglas's *previous novels have all been very popular.*" — *New-York Graphic.*

SYDNIE ADRIANCE;
OR,
TRYING THE WORLD.
12mo. Cloth. $1.50.

"The works of Miss Douglas have stood the test of popular judgment, and be-come the fashion. They are true, natural in delineation, pure and elevating in their tone." — *Express, Easton, Penn.*

Sold by all Booksellers and News-dealers.

LEE AND SHEPARD, Publishers, Boston.

BOOKS OF TRAVEL.

OVER THE OCEAN;
OR,
SIGHTS AND SCENES IN FOREIGN LANDS.

By CURTIS GUILD, editor of "The Boston Commercial Bulletin." Crown 8vo. Cloth. $2.50.

"This is certainly a collection of some of the most perfect pen-pictures of sights and scenes in foreign lands we have ever seen." — *Albion.*

ABROAD AGAIN;
OR,
FRESH FORAYS IN FOREIGN FIELDS.

Uniform with "Over the Ocean." By the same author. Crown 8vo. Cloth. $2.50.

AN AMERICAN GIRL ABROAD.

By Miss ADELINE TRAFTON, author of "His Inheritance," "Katherine Earle," &c. 16mo. Illustrated. $1.50.

"'The American Girl' is a bright, good, merry-hearted girl, off for a good time; and her readers are of the opinion that the journey was a decided success."— *Liberal Christian.*

BEATEN PATHS;
OR,
A WOMAN'S VACATION.

By ELLA W. THOMPSON. 16mo. Cloth. $1.50.

"The author seems to have hit on just the most charming things to see, and talks of them in a charming manner." — *Tribune.*

A THOUSAND MILES' WALK ACROSS SOUTH AMERICA,
OVER THE PAMPAS AND THE ANDES.

By NATHANIEL H. BISHOP. 12mo. Illustrated. $1.50.

VOYAGE OF THE PAPER CANOE.

A Geographical Journey of Twenty-five Hundred Miles from Quebec to the Gulf of Mexico. By the same author. With numerous illustrations and maps specially prepared for this work. Crown 8vo. $2.50.

FOUR MONTHS IN A SNEAK-BOX.

A Boat-Voyage of Twenty-six Hundred Miles down the Ohio and Mississippi Rivers, and along the Gulf of Mexico. By the same author. With numerous maps and illustrations. $2.50.

CAMPS IN THE CARIBBEES.

Being the Adventures of a Naturalist Bird-Hunting in the West India Islands. By FRED A. OBER. Crown 8vo. With maps and illustrations.

Sold by all Booksellers.

LEE AND SHEPARD, Publishers, Boston.

ILLUSTRATED BOOKS.

"THE BREAKING WAVES DASHED HIGH."
(The Pilgrim Fathers.)

By FELICIA HEMANS. Illustrated by Miss L. B. HUMPHREY. 4to. Full gilt. $1.50.

UNIFORM WITH

"NEARER, MY GOD, TO THEE."

By SARAH FLOWER ADAMS. "The well-beloved Sacred Poem." With full-page and initial illustrations. 4to. Full gilt. $1.50.

"OH! WHY SHOULD THE SPIRIT OF MORTAL BE PROUD?"

By WILLIAM KNOX. With full-page and initial illustrations. Uniform with "Nearer, my God, to Thee." Small 4to. Gilt. $1.50.

"ABIDE WITH ME."

By Rev. HENRY FRANCIS LYTE. With full-page and initial illustrations. Uniform with "Nearer, my God, to Thee." 4to. $1.50.

ROCK OF AGES.

By AUG. MONTAGUE TOPLADY. 4to. Illustrated. Full gilt. $1.50.

THE VAGABONDS.

By J. T. TROWBRIDGE. With illustrations by F. O. C. DARLEY. 4to. Cloth. Full gilt. $1.50.

BALLADS OF BEAUTY.

Forty full-page illustrations. 4to. Cloth. $2.50.

BALLADS OF BRAVERY.

Forty full-page illustrations. $2.50.

BALLADS OF HOME.

With 40 full-page illustrations. 4to. Cloth. Full gilt. $2.50.

GEMS OF GENIUS.

Famous Painters and their Pictures. With 40 full-page illustrations. $3.75.

UNIFORM WITH

ART IN CONNECTICUT;
OR,
THE PIONEERS OF ART IN AMERICA.

By H. W. FRENCH. With about 95 portraits and illustrations. $3.75.

ÆSOP'S FABLES.

Illustrated by ERNEST GRISET. A new edition. Upwards of 100 illustrations. 4to. $2.50.

LITTLE PEOPLE OF GOD,
AND WHAT THE POETS HAVE SAID OF THEM.

By Mrs. GEORGE L. AUSTIN. 4to. Illustrated. $2.00.

Sold by all Booksellers.

LEE AND SHEPARD, Publishers, Boston.

ART PUBLICATIONS.

LIVE BOOKS FOR LIVE BOYS.

DONALD'S SCHOOL DAYS.

By Gen. O. O. HOWARD, U.S.A. 16mo, cloth, illustrated. $1.25.

"One of the nicest of the stories for youths which has appeared this season is 'Donald's School Days,' by Gen. O. O. Howard, U.S.A. We should hardly have expected from the gray, one-armed warrior, who commanded an army corps at Chancellorsville, Gettysburg, and under Sherman before Atlanta, a story of American country life which will compare not unfavorably with 'Tom Brown's School Days.'"—*Washington Herald.*

LIVE BOYS;

Or, Charley and Nasho in Texas. 16mo, cloth, illustrated. $1.00.

"The scene of the story is mostly laid in Texas, and with its hunting adventures and descriptions of a herder's life, showing how the great herds of cattle are driven across the prairies to the Northern markets, it is a very interesting book for young people. The two boys who are the heroes of the tale, desirous of visiting the Centennial, manage by trapping, hunting, and herding, to secure the necessary means; and the pluck and perseverance shown by them is characteristic of frontier life, where every one has to depend on his own abilities." — *New-England Farmer.*

IKE PARTINGTON;

Or, The Adventures of a Human Boy and His Friends. By B. P. SHILLABER (Mrs. Partington). 16mo. cloth, illustrated. $1.25.

"Were there a civilized nation on the face of the earth whose people have not heard of our Mother Partington's son 'Ike,' or even did we for a moment suppose there existed a solitary individual from Maine to the Gulf, or the Atlantic to the Pacific, ignorant of 'Ike's' existence, we might feel inclined to say something in behalf of this book. With a world-wide fame, however, it is needless. His name is the synonyme for fun, the world over; and to say that a reading of his book is the best remedy for general debility known, must be a sufficient indorsement to give it an immense sale."— *American Monthly, Philadelphia.*

PIZARRO:

His Adventures and Conquests. By GEORGE M. TOWLE. 16mo, handsomely illustrated. $1.00.

"The exciting career of this great Spanish captain is familiar to all; but previous authors have generally failed to clothe the story with that easy familiar style so attractive to the young. Mr. Towle has succeeded in striking the happy medium between dry details and romantic exuberance in his 'Pizarro.' His story opens with a graphic picture of the young Pizarro's boy life; and the author carries the reader on, step by step, with the career of the adventurous youth, until the conquest of Peru is completed." — *New-Haven Register.*

VASCO DA GAMA:

His Voyages and Adventures. By GEORGE M. TOWLE. 16mo, illustrated. $1.00.

These two volumes are the pioneers of a series of "Heroes of History."

"It will be remembered that Da Gama was in his day more famous than Columbus, and that he discovered the way to India around the Cape of Good Hope. His life was brimful of adventure, and the book will be of great interest to the young for whom it is especially prepared, yet not the less interesting to older people who love history, and the deeds of brave men when the earth was much younger than at present. It is illustrated and well printed." — *Taunton Gazette.*

Sold by all Booksellers and Newsdealers, and sent by mail, postpaid, on receipt of price.

LEE & SHEPARD, Publishers . . . . Boston.
C. T. DILLINGHAM . . . . New York.

5